THE UNITED STATES AND THE PHILIPPINES

AEI-Hoover
policy studies

The studies in this series are issued jointly
by the American Enterprise Institute
for Public Policy Research and the Hoover
Institution on War, Revolution and Peace.
They are designed to focus on
policy problems of current and future interest,
to set forth the factors underlying
these problems and to evaluate
courses of action available to policy makers.
The views expressed in these studies
are those of the authors and do not necessarily
reflect the views of the staff, officers
or members of the governing boards of
AEI or the Hoover Institution.

THE UNITED STATES AND THE PHILIPPINES

Background for policy

Claude A. Buss

American Enterprise Institute for Public Policy Research
Washington, D. C.
Hoover Institution on War, Revolution and Peace
Stanford University, Stanford, California

Library of Congress Cataloging in Publication Data

Buss, Claude Albert.
  The United States and the Philippines.

  (AEI-Hoover policy studies ; 23) (Hoover Institute studies ; 59)
  1. United States—Foreign relations—Philippine Islands. 2. Philippine
Islands—Foreign relations—United States. I. Title. II. Series. III. Series:
Hoover Institution studies ; 59.
E183.8.P5B87   327.73'0599   77-22589
ISBN 0-8447-3258-3

AEI-Hoover policy studies 23; Hoover Institution Studies 59

Printed in the United States of America

Contents

Preface

Since the proclamation of martial law in the Republic of the Philippines and the end of U.S. involvement in Indochina, relations between the United States and the Philippines, once taken for granted as friendly and cooperative, have become touchy and contentious. Understanding why and how this change has taken place and achieving a satisfactory solution of the issues dividing the two countries are prerequisites for peace and stability with progress in Southeast Asia and the Western Pacific.

This study is divided into three parts, showing the evolution of American policy and the roots of conflict before Ferdinand Marcos came to power in the Philippines, the evolution of Philippine policy during the Marcos years before and after martial law, and the progressive reexamination of American interests and policy since the withdrawal from Vietnam and the pronouncement of the Nixon Doctrine. Attention is focused on the central issues of security, economics, and good will.

Throughout the period when sovereignty over the Philippines was exercised by the United States, Americans looked upon the Philippines as indispensable to their interests and policies in East Asia. The security interest was measured in terms of the diplomatic role of the United States in all East Asia, and the economic value of the Philippines was inflated by the proximity of the islands to the China market. In addition, the careful transplanting of political ideals and the democratic form of government from the United States to the Philippines forged a cultural and emotional bond.

Although U.S.-Philippine relations appeared placid on the surface, they were ruffled from the beginning by the grievances of Filipino leaders. Relieved of the yoke of Spain, the Filipinos wanted to be free. They had their own philosophy, political organizations, democratic form of government, even their own heroes, but to all of these the Americans were indifferent. For nearly half a century under American rule the Filipinos enjoyed an enlightened colonial administration and made great progress toward self-government, but they felt increasing resentment over their political and economic subservience to the United States. The demand for independence grew louder.

Dissatisfaction with colonial status in the Philippines was matched by a continuing debate in the United States between those who were pleased with the American experience in the Philippines and those who advocated independence, primarily on ideological grounds. The arguments reached a climax with the Great Depression, when certain American economic interests added their support to the pro-independence faction, hoping to reduce foreign competition by making the Philippines independent, and thus eliminating its favored status in matters of trade. The U.S. Congress responded in 1934 by legislating a timetable for independence and establishing the Philippine Commonwealth. Although interrupted by World War II and the Japanese occupation of the Philippines, the transition from colony to independent nation was effected, as promised, on July 4, 1946.

During the 1950s, the United States and the new Republic of the Philippines forged close ties as allies in the cold war. They concluded a Mutual Defense Treaty and the United States inaugurated substantial programs of military and economic assistance. The first indications of differences appeared when the United States began to ask whether its commitment to the Philippines was excessively costly and perhaps counterproductive. Questions being raised in the Philippines, meanwhile, implied the insufficiency of the American commitment and the disproportion between the benefits flowing to the two parties from the economic relationship. The continuance of good will was threatened by the rising demands of Filipino nationalists, which contained ominous undertones of anti-Americanism.

Mutual recriminations were subdued as long as the United States coveted the Philippines as a principal supporter of its anti-Communist policies in Asia and as long as those policies promised to be successful. With the dramatic turn of events in Vietnam, both Manila and Washington plunged into a fundamental reappraisal of their national interests and foreign policies. The Philippines struck out in new directions to reduce its military and economic dependence on the United States and strengthened its diplomatic hand by the proclamation of martial law. It undertook a reexamination of its Mutual Defense Treaty with the United States, sought further changes in the agreements on U.S. bases and the military assistance program, and entered into negotiations covering the status of American investments in the Philippines and the conditions of U.S.-Philippine trade after the expiration of the Laurel-Langley agreement in 1974. The Philippines intensified its drive for self-reliance and increased its efforts to convert Southeast Asia into a zone of peace, freedom, and neutrality. It pursued policies of détente with the Socialist-Communist states, including the Soviet Union and the People's Republic of China, taking care, however, to leave the door wide open for good relations with the United States. For all the nationalistic rhetoric about the heritage of imperialism and the colonial mentality, a good Philippine-American relationship was still considered essential to the best interests of the Philippines.

After the withdrawal from Vietnam, the opening gambit in détente with China, and the pronouncement of the Nixon Doctrine, Americans in both the executive and legislative branches of government undertook a reexamination of national priorities in Southeast Asia and the Western Pacific. Because the maintenance of credibility remained foremost among its priorities, the administration continued to profess its fidelity to the commitments it had already made. It gave assurances to the Philippines that it would abide by the Mutual Defense Treaty, and would work out mutually acceptable modifications to the bases agreement and the military assistance program. It would also negotiate a new treaty of commercial relations and economic development, if desired, to replace the system of special relations that expired in 1974. But in view of its determination to maintain a lower profile and to avoid another Vietnam, it would have to reconsider how far it could go in continuing assistance to a government that, although friendly, had dismantled democracy and violated human rights. With the succession of President Carter to the White House, the administration continued to place high priority on the maintenance of good will between the United States and the Philippines in spite of its emphasis on human rights.

The author here wishes to acknowledge his special gratitude to Joanne Lewinsohn, Milton Meyer, Lela Noble, Robert Bowers, Mike Onorato, Gerald Wheeler, and many other fellow students of Philippine affairs who must be unnamed. They are, of course, in no way responsible for any of his statements or mistakes. He owes particular thanks to the Hoover Institution on War, Revolution and Peace and to the American Enterprise Institute for Public Policy Research under whose grant this study was undertaken.

Palo Alto, California
September 1977

1

The United States
and the Philippines, 1896-1965

The Roots of American Policy

From May 1, 1898, when Commodore Dewey defeated the Spanish fleet in Manila Bay, until July 4, 1946, when President Truman proclaimed the end of American sovereignty in the Philippines, the United States regarded the Philippines as its outpost in the far Pacific. During this period important decisions affecting the Philippines were made in Washington. Should the 1898 war against Spain in Cuba be extended to the Philippines? Should the entire Philippine archipelago be annexed as a consequence of victory? Should a civil government be installed after the close of military operations and, if so, when? How should the Philippines be administered in accordance with the philosophy and principles of the majority party in the United States? How could opportunities for self-government in the Philippines be expanded? How should the Philippines be prepared for independence and when should independence be granted? Controversial questions like these were decided by Americans, with an eye to the rights and interests of the United States.

By 1898 considerations of strategy and commerce had combined to produce a new American outlook on world affairs that was specifically applicable to the Philippines. Its prophet was Captain Alfred T. Mahan, who wrote that a nation, to be great, must have not only land power but also sea power to expand its shipping and protect its commerce. America, he argued, must look outward, must search for distant markets and sources of raw materials. It must acquire a large merchant marine, a powerful navy, safe ports and coaling stations, naval

1

bases around the world, and colonies.[1] According to Mahan, expansion was natural, necessary, and irrepressible, and a throng of neoimperialists agreed. Their thoughts came to focus on the China market—and a way station in the Philippines.[2]

After the declaration of war against Spain, Commodore Dewey was ordered to proceed at once to the Philippines and commence operations against the Spanish fleet.[3] He won the Battle of Manila Bay on May 1, 1898, and after receiving adequate reinforcements he pushed on to occupy the city of Manila on August 13, 1898, only hours after the Spanish government in Madrid had agreed to a cease-fire. Negotiations for peace concluded with the signing of the Treaty of Paris on December 10, 1898. Spain ceded the Philippines to the United States in return for the payment of $20 million and the admission of Spanish ships and merchandise to the Philippines for a ten-year period on the same terms as the ships and merchandise of the United States. The treaty was approved by the U.S. Senate, and the Philippines became American territory on February 6, 1899.[4]

The war against Spain was only part of the Philippine story. Long before the Americans entered the picture, the Philippines seethed with protest against Spanish rule. Some Filipinos objected to what they felt was abuse and discrimination under colonial domination. A small group of brilliant Filipino writers in Spain, the best known of whom was José Rizal, voiced their demands for better treatment and gave impetus to an embryonic Philippine nationalism. In the Philippines more impetuous "sons of the soil," as they called themselves, revolted openly against the Spanish administration. In 1897 the rebel leaders were bought off by the Spanish and exiled to Hong Kong where they pushed on with their plots to overthrow their Spanish masters. When the United States declared war on Spain, these Filipino leaders estab-

---

1 Alfred T. Mahan, *Influence of Sea Power Upon History, 1660-1783* (Boston: Little, Brown and Co., 1890), especially Chapter 1, "Discussion of the Elements of Sea Power."

2 Thomas J. McCormick, *China Market: America's Quest for Informal Empire, 1893-1901* (Chicago: Quadrangle Books, 1967). Contains an excellent bibliographical note.

3 A. Whitney Griswold, *Far Eastern Policy of the United States* (New York: Harcourt, Brace, 1938), p. 13.

4 Fred L. Israel, ed., *Major Peace Treaties of Modern History* (New York: Chelsea House Publishers, 1967), p. 851.

lished contacts with the Americans, hoping for cooperative action against a common enemy. According to General Emilio Aguinaldo, the most famous among them, Dewey said there was no doubt that the United States would recognize Philippine independence.[5]

Shortly after the Battle of Manila Bay, General Aguinaldo was brought to the Philippines on board an American transport. He established himself at Cavite, outside Manila and not far from Dewey's headquarters, and on June 12, 1898, proclaimed the independence of the Philippine Republic and hoisted the Philippine flag. He formed a revolutionary government and sent a committee abroad to seek arms and diplomatic recognition. Frustrated by his virtual exclusion from the American occupation of the city of Manila, Aguinaldo assembled a revolutionary Congress in nearby Malolos on September 15, 1898. This Congress adopted a constitution anticipating its own jurisdiction over an independent Philippines.[6]

American military rule was proclaimed in Manila immediately after the surrender of the city by the Spanish, and on December 21, 1898, military control was extended over the entire archipelago.[7] This deepened the bitterness of the revolutionary leaders, who objected to the transfer of sovereignty from Spain to the United States. On February 4, 1899, hostilities in the Philippines broke out between Filipino and American forces, just prior to the ratification of the Treaty of Paris. Thus from the outset, the American administration was faced with insurgency. When the Americans denied the Filipinos their independence, insurrection was inevitable. It raged throughout the islands, primarily in Luzon. Hostilities continued until 1902, and cost the Americans more than 4,000 killed in action, nearly 3,000 wounded, and three times as much money as the war against Spain. The Filipinos lost 16,000 killed in action and 200,000 dead from hunger and disease.[8]

While military rule was still in force and guerrilla fighting was still going on, the Americans prepared for the transition to civil administra-

[5] Teodoro A. Agoncillo and Oscar M. Alfonso, *Short History of the Filipino People* (Manila: University of the Philippines, 1960), p. 235.
[6] See Teodoro A. Agoncillo, *Malolos, The Crisis of the Republic* (Quezon City: University of the Philippines, 1960), Chapters 7 and 8 for a Filipino account sympathetic to Aguinaldo, and Dean C. Worcester, *The Philippines, Past and Present* (New York: Macmillan, 1930), pp. 192-209 for a point of view which is less laudatory.
[7] George A. Malcolm and Maximo M. Kalaw, *Philippine Government* (New York: D. C. Heath and Co., 1923), p. 72.
[8] Pedro S. de Achutegui, S.J. and Miguel A. Bernad, S.J., *Religious Revolution in the Philippines* (Manila: Ateneo de Manila, 1960), p. 35.

tion and laid down the fundamental lines of colonial policy. In March 1899, President McKinley sent a commission under President Jacob Gould Schurman of Cornell University to facilitate the most humane, pacific, and effective extension of authority and to secure with the least possible delay the benefits of a wise and generous protection to life and property. The commission was to make recommendations for the well-being of the Philippine people and their elevation and advancement to a position among the most civilized peoples of the world. It was to be made clear that the Americans desired nothing for themselves but would hold the archipelago as a trust in the sole interest of the Philippine people.[9]

The recommendations of the Schurman Commission constituted an enlightened statement of the American concept of the colonial mission. The Schurman Commission recommended the establishment of a civilian administration under an American governor, cabinet, and advisory council, with an effective civil service to be staffed by Filipinos in ever-increasing numbers. The United States should establish elementary and higher schools, the commission said, and should guarantee the rights and liberties of Filipinos, including freedom of religious worship. The Philippines should be administered financially for the benefit of the people and the development of the country. Self-government should be the ultimate goal, but independence was out of the question in the immediate future for the good of the people themselves.[10]

Acting on these recommendations, President McKinley in April 1900 instructed a second commission under William Howard Taft to establish a government in the Philippines designed for the happiness, peace, and prosperity of the people of the Philippine Islands and conforming to their customs, their habits, and even their prejudices. The Taft Commission was given no mandate to grant or promise independence but was to set up a just and effective government within the limits of the great American principles of government deemed essential to the rule of law and the maintenance of individual freedom. Such principles included the complete separation of church and state, regard

[9] U.S. Congress, Senate, *Report of the Philippine Commission,* 56th Congress, 1st session, Senate Document No. 138, 1900; hereinafter referred to as *Schurman Report.* Instructions to the commission are in vol. 1, p. 185.

[10] Ibid., pp. 82-84.

4

for the importance and dignity of the individual, respect for private property, and public education.[11]

Legislative power was transferred to Taft and the members of his commission, and on July 4, 1901, Taft was named the first civil governor of the Philippines. Within a year, three Filipinos were added to the Philippine Commission and Filipinos were employed at every administrative level.

In July 1902, the Congress of the United States passed the Cooper Bill, the first Philippine Organic Act, legalizing all measures regarding the Philippines previously taken by the executive branch of the government and recognizing the Philippines as unincorporated U.S. territory. All residents of the islands who were Spanish subjects were entitled to become citizens of the Philippines but not of the United States. The act provided for a bicameral legislature, with the Philippine Commission as the upper house and a lower house to be elected within two years after the restoration of peace and order and the publication of a national census. Rules were laid down for the exploitation of natural resources and the granting of franchises for public service. Limits were placed on the acquisition of public lands. The act also set up the Bureau of Insular Affairs in the War Department as the official administrative agency and authorized the Philippines to send two resident commissioners to Washington with the right to speak but not to vote in the U.S. Congress.[12]

Colonial Administration American Style

The U.S. colonial administration of the Philippines passed through three distinct periods: from 1902 to 1913, the Republican era dominated by William Howard Taft, from 1913 to 1921, the Democratic interregnum of Woodrow Wilson; and from 1921 to 1933, a generally Republican period under Warren G. Harding, Calvin Coolidge, and Herbert Hoover, followed by two years under Franklin D. Roosevelt, which, with the establishment of the Philippine Commonwealth, brought the colonial period to its close.

---

[11] U.S. Congress, House of Representatives, *Annual Report of the War Department for the Fiscal Year Ended June 30, 1900*, 56th Congress, 2nd session, House Document No. 2, 1900. The instructions to the Taft Commission are on p. 72.

[12] U.S., *Statutes at Large*, 57th Congress, vol. 32, part 1, pp. 691-712.

The Formative Years. Throughout the first period of the American era in the Philippines, it was generally accepted that colonial possession of the Philippines was in the American national interest. The strategic importance of the archipelago loomed ever larger as American naval power grew and the Pacific became more and more an American lake. German interests in the Pacific were also rising, and Japanese power in East Asia and the Western Pacific was growing rapidly. From the Philippines, where the American armed forces had their best training ground and most prestigious outpost, these developments could be observed and evaluated. The location of the Philippines also helped keep alive American faith in the open door of commercial opportunity in China and added a certain reality to the announced American intention to support the international status quo. The Philippines seemed vital to the emergence of the United States as a first-class world power.

The first task of the American administration was to restore law and order and to lay the foundations for peaceful progress. Security was provided by the U.S. navy and the stationing of U.S. army units in bases throughout the country. A special unit was created known as the Philippine Scouts, in which the enlisted men were Filipinos and the officers were American regulars. In addition, the Philippine Constabulary, a national police force, was established.

Within a decade, significant progress was made in secularizing the government and the schools. The existing Spanish legal system was modified to accommodate American concepts based on the common law. Civil rights and equality before the law were guaranteed and an independent judiciary was created on the American pattern. Filipinos were admitted to the civil service in the lower ranks. Popular election of Filipino officials was introduced at the local level and the formation of political parties was permitted. In 1907, the Nacionalista party, the champion of immediate independence, won control of the first popularly elected National Assembly.

A system of public education from the primary grades to the University of the Philippines was established with instruction carried out in the English language. In matters of economic development, the infrastructure of currency and finance was put on a sound basis. Improvements were made in harbor facilities, railways, streets, highways, and public utilities. Contracts were let for the exploitation of mines, forests, and other natural resources. Tremendous strides were made in improving sanitary conditions and public health. Although

6

self-government and national unity were promoted, neither Taft nor the Republicans generally believed that the Philippines was ready for independence.[13]

As soon as the treaty guarantee of equal treatment for Spanish subjects and merchandise expired in 1909, the Philippines was incorporated into the free market of the United States. It was this new tariff legislation that made the Philippines attractive for American investment and business activity and that accounted for the substantial growth of U.S.-Philippine international trade.

By this legislation American goods were allowed to enter the Philippines duty-free and goods from the Philippines were given the same privilege in the United States. This arrangement was beneficial for some, but not all, of the parties concerned. It was helpful for exporters in the respective countries and for those consumers who appreciated cheaper prices. On the other hand, it was damaging to local producers who were obliged to compete against the favored importers. For example, American sugar growers, dairy interests, and cigar makers did not relish the enhanced competition from the Philippine sugar, coconut oil, and tobacco exporters, whether they were of Philippine, American, or any other nationality. Likewise, domestic interests in the Philippines complained that they were deprived of the opportunity for industrialization because of the availability of U.S. manufactured goods. Certainly the new tariff policy added to the complications of the land problems in the Philippines. It encouraged large land holdings rather than small farms, for capital crops and the assurance of an American market took away much of the incentive for improved methods of agricultural production.[14]

In these early formative years of American colonial policy, the enormity of the task of molding a Filipino nation in the American image became very clear. No American involved in the process of transplanting democracy into the alien, tropical soil of Asia—whether government

[13] Garel A. Grunder and William E. Livezey, *The Philippines and the United States* (Norman, Oklahoma: University of Oklahoma Press, 1951), especially Chapter 5, "Governing the Philippines, 1902-1913," pp. 84-103. See also Peter W. Stanley, *A Nation in the Making* (Cambridge: Harvard University Press, 1974), Part 2, "The Philippines and the United States, 1899-1912," especially pp. 82-114, and Agoncillo and Alfonso, *Short History of the Filipino People,* p. 298 ff.

[14] U.S., *Statutes at Large,* 61st Congress, *Philippine Tariff Law,* vol. 36, part 1, pp. 130-178, and pp. 83-85 for Section 5 of Payne Aldrich Tariff Law referring to Philippine Islands.

official, businessman, lawyer, or teacher—doubted the value of the objective or minimized the difficulties of achieving it. The Filipino people, all 7 million of them, were diverse in language, mostly illiterate, and completely unprepared for the idea of governing themselves. Their loyalties were to family, village, or at most a province or an island. From pre-Spanish days they had become accustomed to class distinctions, and for 300 years under Spain they had been denied participation in government at the national level. It would take time to modify the underlying native social customs and structure and the political practices and institutions inherited from Spain. Thus, the policies of education, encouragement of national unity, economic development, and promotion of self-government were implemented under a stern and uncompromising American tutelage.[15]

One of the most difficult problems that the Americans faced from the outset and which grew more complex with the passing of the years was the treatment of the Muslims, or Moros, in the southern islands. These people, though they constituted only 4 percent of the population, inhabited 40 percent of the entire land area of the Philippines. They were of the same ethnic stock as the Christian Filipinos but differed from them in both culture and religion, living in distinct tribes— Maguindanaos, Maranaos, Yakans, Samals, Sulus, and so on—and ruled by their hereditary chieftains without benefit of written laws. Converted to Islam before the arrival of Magellan in 1519, the Moros had never been conquered by the Spanish, and the Americans made no effort to subdue them. They had a deserved reputation for fierceness and a willingness to die rather than surrender.

American authority was established in Mindanao and the neighboring islands in 1899 and was exercised by a military commander who was at the same time a civil administrator. An agreement was worked out whereby the principal Moro authority, the sultan of Jolo, recognized the sovereignty of the United States in return for American recognition of his spiritual prerogatives. The sultan and some of the leading chieftains, or *datus,* were paid monthly stipends by the American authorities. American policy was to extend roads, schools, and all

---

[15] The problems, philosophy, and achievements of Americans in the Philippines are usefully discussed by three of the best known administrators themselves. See W. Cameron Forbes, *The Philippine Islands*, 2 vols. (Boston: Houghton Mifflin, 1928); Dean C. Worcester, *The Philippines, Past and Present*, 2 vols. (New York: Macmillan, 1914); and Joseph Ralston Hayden, *The Philippines* (New York: Macmillan, 1947).

the benefits of the American administration to the Moros as well as to the Christian Filipinos. Little support was given to the formation of a separate Muslim state; rather, it was assumed that the Moros would take their place in a united self-governing Philippine nation. Nevertheless, constant disorder in the Moro areas obliged the Americans to take harsh measures for the preservation of law and order, although the monthly payments to the Moro dignitaries continued.

Strict military administration of the Moro islands continued until 1912, when it was replaced by civil government under an American. In 1916 the Philippine legislature assumed responsibility for Moro affairs and the executive authority was lodged in the Bureau of Non-Christian Tribes in the governor general's office. By that time Christian Filipinos had begun to move from the more densely populated northern islands into the southern islands, and controversies over land settlement had become a far more pressing issue than the religious and cultural differences in relations between Christians and Moros.[16]

Another problem that plagued American policy makers from the beginning was agrarian unrest. Manageable at first, it reached the proportions of insurgency after World War II. It seemed paradoxical that agrarian unrest should exist at all in the Philippines, with its fertile soil, abundant rainfall, and lack of population pressure. Land was the basis of wealth, and agriculture was the way of life for 75 percent of the population.

Before the coming of the Spanish, life in the Philippines had centered on the family and the village. Land holding had been a community affair, with crop distribution depending upon status within the society. Class distinctions had been recognized, but social stability had been preserved by a complex system of feudal and kinship obligations. Each family, village, and tribe had operated within its own familiar peasant world according to its own customs and beliefs.

Indigenous patterns were modified but not erased by the Spanish conquest. A central government and a religious hierarchy were superimposed on the peasant world. All land was claimed by the conqueror and the title to its use was distributed, for pay or favor, to landlords great and small. The landlord-tenant relationship became the key to individual prosperity and social stability. The *cacique,* or local aristocrat, became the pillar of the Spanish edifice at the local level and the point of contact between the peasants and the government authorities.

---

[16] Grunder and Livezey, *The Philippines and the United States*, pp. 137-145.

The welfare of the landlord was identified with that of the Spanish rulers, not that of the peasants.

While landlords prospered, tenants and landless agricultural workers suffered. Peasants could not protest without running afoul of the local police, who were the agents of the landlords. They could not complain, for neither the landlord nor the government would hear. Agrarian unrest in Spanish times was limited to secret societies, banditry, or isolated, fanatical religious movements. But when the rebellion against Spain occurred in the 1890s, it was the peasants who flocked to the revolutionary army in the belief that in fighting against Spain they were fighting against the established socioeconomic order.[17]

These were the seeds of agrarian unrest the Americans inherited. The tenants fought against the United States just as they had fought against Spain. When the insurrection was over, they had to return to the rice plots that they had abandoned and hope that the United States would not champion the landlords as the Spanish had done. The dilemma that the Americans faced was how to win the aristocratic, leadership elements to the cooperative task of nation building and at the same time promote the welfare of the neglected peasant masses. The latter task proved to be far more baffling than the former.

The Americans chose not to destroy the old Spanish landholding system, which was the product of more than three centuries of experience. Improvements in landlord-tenant relationships would have to be accomplished within the existing system and slowly, by patient administration safeguarding the peasants rights and by popular education. The first small step was the purchase of some 410,000 acres of "friar lands"—lands owned by religious orders—around Manila for the purpose of redistributing them to their tenant cultivators. The redistribution process proved to be long, costly, and disappointing. Subsequently, the peasant masses were neglected by the Americans, who showed great concern for the sophisticated and well-to-do in the Philippines—the traders, landlords, lawyers, political leaders, and the new middle class—but little for tenants and landless rural workers. The wretched lot of the poor became progressively worse as the cost of living rose and population pressure increased. The root causes of agrarian unrest were allowed to grow in the early years of the American administration.

---

[17] David R. Sturtevant, "Philippine Social Structure and its Relation to Agrarian Unrest," a detailed study of the origins of agrarian unrest in the Philippines (unpublished Ph.D. dissertation, Stanford University, 1958).

Preparing for Independence. The Democrats, who were in power from 1913 to 1921, were more responsive to the sentiments of the Filipinos than the Republicans had been, but they too had accepted the idea that the retention of the Philippines was good for the national interest. In 1913 President Wilson appointed Francis Burton Harrison governor general. Upon Harrison's arrival in Manila, he announced that all future U.S. policies would have independence as their ultimate objective and that this would be promoted as rapidly as the safety and the permanent interests of the islands permitted.

The intention of the Democratic administration was to grant the Philippines as much power over domestic affairs as was possible without impairing the sovereignty of the United States. Filipinos were given a five-to-four majority on the Philippine Commission and were named to the newly created Council of State and Board of Control for government corporations. Filipinos were appointed to replace Americans in a deliberate move to nationalize the civil service, and the American governor general came very close to surrendering his leadership role to the rising young Nacionalista party politicians Sergio Osmena and Manuel Quezon.[18]

In 1916 Congress passed the Jones Law, which was to remain the authoritative statement of American policy for the next nineteen years.[19] This law provided for significant changes in the organization and rights of the government of the Philippines, but its major import was contained in the preamble. This stated that the purpose of the United States was to withdraw its sovereignty and recognize the independence of the Philippines as soon as a stable government could be established therein. Former President Taft, speaking for the Republicans, opposed the Jones Bill, calling it cruel to the Filipinos and shameful to Americans. By moving too fast, Taft charged, the United States would make the Filipinos mere flotsam in the sea of Oriental politics.

It was not until after the First World War that the administration recommended to Congress the granting of Philippine independence. Both President Wilson and Governor General Harrison stated that the

---

[18] Francis Burton Harrison, *Cornerstone of Philippine Independence* (New York: Century, 1932). For an appraisal of Democratic policies see Michael P. Onorato, *Francis B. Harrison: Origins of the Philippine Republic* (Ithaca: Cornell University, 1974).

[19] U.S., *Statutes at Large*, 64th Congress, vol. 39, part 1, pp. 545-556.

necessary condition—the establishment of stable government—had been fulfilled. By that time, the Republicans were back in control of Congress, however, and saw retrogression rather than stability in the Philippines. They blamed the Democrats for an empty treasury and appalling political and economic deterioration in the Philippines.[20]

From 1921 to 1934 the Philippines was administered under the Jones Law, but in a new spirit. Shortly after Harding was elected President, he sent General Leonard Wood and former Governor General W. Cameron Forbes to the Philippines to study and report on the probable effects of independence on the Philippines, with special attention to the financial situation of the people and government, the ability of the existing government to perform its function efficiently, its treatment of the backward people of the islands, and the ability of the Filipinos to defend their territory from the land-hungry peoples who surrounded them (presumably the Japanese).[21]

Wood and Forbes found the people happy, peaceful, and keenly appreciative of the benefits of American rule, but wrote, "the experience of the past eight years . . . has not been such as to justify the people of the United States in relinquishing supervision of the government of the Philippine Islands, withdrawing their army and navy, and leaving the islands a prey to any powerful nation coveting their rich soil and potential commercial advantages."[22] Wood and Forbes believed that premature withdrawal would be a betrayal of the Philippine people, an obstruction of progress, and a discreditable neglect of national duty.[23]

General Wood was persuaded to accept the governor generalship, and he spent the last six years of his life, from 1921 to 1927, seeking the greater educational, cultural, economic, and political advances that he believed necessary before the Filipinos could undertake full responsibility for their government. Wood clashed continually and bitterly with Manuel Quezon, who had become the undisputed leader of the

---

[20] U.S. Congress, Senate Committee on Philippines and House Committee on Insular Affairs, *Hearings on Philippine Independence, Joint Hearing*, 66th Congress, 1st session. Selections from these hearings may also be found in *House Report 709*, part 2, 68th Congress, 1st session. Governor General Harrison's report for 1920 is in House Document 267, 67th Congress, 2nd session, pp. 1-3. The views of leading Republicans are further elaborated in the Wood-Forbes report cited in note 21.

[21] U.S. Congress, *House Document, No. 398*, 67th Congress, 2nd session, "Report of the Governor General, 1921," pp. 14-17.

[22] Ibid., pp. 42-43.

[23] Ibid., p. 43.

Philippine nationalists, over respective prerogatives in appointments, control of government corporations, limitations on private American investments in the Philippines, public expenditures, and the independence issue. Wood was determined to maintain the primacy of the American executive over the Philippine legislature, restore financial solvency to the government, and reestablish administrative efficiency. Independence, Wood thought, was a generation in the future, while Quezon sought immediate independence in accord with the American promise as he construed it.[24]

While the American administration and the Philippine political leaders quarreled, both neglected the unrepresented minorities—the needy classes consisting of urban laborers, tenant farmers, renters who rented land for a fixed sum rather than a share of the crop, and landless agricultural workers, who had no spokesman for their interests. Their poverty, ignorance, and superstition made them highly receptive to antigovernment propaganda. These were the people who had risen against their Spanish tyrants, who had formed the bulk of the army of the short-lived Philippine Republic of 1898, and who had resisted annexation by the United States. Unable to improve their wretched lot by the ballot, they were ready to resort to bullets and bolos.

In 1923 and 1924, a subversive group known as Colorums attacked the constabulary and government buildings in Mindanao and Luzon, but they were easily suppressed. In the early thirties a school teacher who had been dismissed founded a secret society called the Sakdalistas (after the Tagalog word *sakdal* meaning to strike). Eventually the Sakdalistas grew so bold as to publish their own newspaper and run their own candidates for public office. Their platform called for complete, absolute, and immediate independence; opposition to Philippine oligarchs and their American supporters; and establishment of a national government of the poor, for the poor, and by the poor. On the night of May 2–3, 1935, they stormed government buildings in fourteen towns in the neighborhood of Manila. As many as 68,000 peasants

---

[24] Grunder and Livezey, *The Philippines and the United States,* Chapter 10, "The Regime of Leonard Wood," pp. 162-183, gives a good account of Wood's administration. For further details, see Hermann Hagedorn, *Leonard Wood, a Biography,* 2 vols. (New York: Harper and Brothers, 1931) and Manuel Quezon, *The Good Fight* (New York: D. Appleton-Century Company, 1946). President Quezon once remarked to the author, "My fight with General Wood sent him to his grave and me to Monrovia" (a sanatorium in Southern California).

may have been involved, but their uprising, disorganized and badly led, was put down immediately by the government forces.[25]

The cause of the underprivileged masses was a challenge to the Socialists and Communists who aspired to lead the movement. In 1929 a distinguished lawyer, Pedro Abad Santos, organized a Socialist party in Pampanga province, Luzon, where the countryside was controlled by landlords who ruled with an iron hand, and some of whom had their own private armies. Luis Taruc, later the leader of the insurgents, was among those who joined Santos. In 1930 Crisanto Evangelista, with the help and advice of American and Indonesian Communists and the Comintern, founded the Communist party of the Philippines, which attracted trade union leaders, lower-middle-class clerical workers, and student activists. Because of strikes and other labor troubles, the Communist party was banned in 1931 and Evangelista was sentenced to eight years in jail.[26] It was already apparent that the government would face a serious threat if the aggrieved classes in the countryside and in the city should join forces, particularly if they were mobilized under the capable, fanatical leadership that the Socialists or Communists might provide.

But there were no further outbreaks of serious civil disorder for a few years, and successive governors general after Wood—Henry L. Stimson, Dwight Davis, and Theodore Roosevelt, Jr.—achieved a creditable record of economic development. Their major concerns were the security interests of the United States involving the Philippines and the issue of independence. They shared the standard Republican convictions that immediate independence would bring political and economic chaos to the islands, betray the historical American commitment to the Philippines, injure trade in the Far East, and complicate international relations in that area.[27] As long as the Republicans were in office, they felt that the protection of worldwide American interests and of international stability in the Far East depended upon a strong American navy and continued American guardianship of the Philippines. The rise of restless Japan was seen as a potential threat. Mean-

---

[25] Hayden, *The Philippines,* Chapter 15, "The Unrepresented Minority," pp. 376-400. Dr. Hayden's account is authoritative. He was vice-governor of the Philippines from 1933 to 1935.

[26] Jean Grossholtz, *The Philippines* (Boston: Little, Brown and Co., 1964), pp. 29-30. See also Justus M. Van der Kroef, "The Philippines," in *Yearbook on International Communist Affairs* (Stanford: Hoover Institution Press, 1976), pp. 359-371.

[27] Their views are clearly expressed in the successive annual reports of the governor general of the Philippine Islands to the secretary of war.

while agitation increased, both in the Philippines and the United States, for changes in the U.S.-Philippine relationship. Filipinos campaigned more fervently for immediate independence and some Americans began to think of the Philippines as more of a liability than an asset. They wondered whether the granting of independence might be a good way of shedding a political responsibility and eliminating the economic advantages enjoyed by Philippine products in the American market.

After the stock market crash in 1929, congressmen from the farm states, backed by such powerful organizations as the National Grange, the National Dairy Union, and the American Farm Bureau Federation, increased their efforts for Philippine independence. To them, Philippine independence would mean higher taxes on coconut oil, which would increase the price of margarine and benefit the market for real butter. American sugar, tobacco, and cordage interests, too, supported independence, and the American Federation of Labor made efforts to have Filipinos classified as "other Oriental immigrants," which would give American wage earners on the West Coast added protection against cheap foreign competition.[28] All the forces making for independence came together with the election of Franklin D. Roosevelt in 1932. The only remaining question was the exact manner in which the American colonial administration would be brought to an end.

The Philippine Commonwealth

In March 1934, the new Democratic Congress passed the Tydings-McDuffie Act, the first organic act since the Jones Law. This became the blueprint for Philippine independence. The act provided for a ten-year transitional period, at the end of which the Philippines was to be given outright independence. During the transition, the interests of the United States would be entrusted to a high commissioner, who would replace the former governor general. The affairs of the Philippines would be placed in the hands of a Commonwealth government, to be established by a constitution of the Philippine people's own making. The United States reserved the right to review Philippine court decisions, limit the Philippine public debt and foreign loans, maintain military and naval reservations, keep armed forces in the Philippines,

---

[28] Grayson Kirk, *Philippine Independence* (New York: Farrar and Rinehart, 1936), especially Chapter 4, "The Farm Groups Take a Hand," pp. 73-101. The appendix to this study includes the text of the Tydings-McDuffie Act and the constitution of the Philippines.

and intervene for the preservation of the government of the Common-wealth or for the protection of life, property, and individual liberty.

Looking toward Philippine economic independence, the Tydings-McDuffie law established a system of duty-free quotas and graduated tariffs to cushion the shocks of adjustment. Specific quotas on sugar, coconut oil, and abaca (Manila hemp), for example, were to remain effective for five years, after which the benefits of the quotas would be reduced by gradually increasing tariff levies.[29]

The new Philippine constitution drafted by the 1935 constitutional convention contained a few features that were distinctively Filipino. The constitution was based on the idea of the superiority of the state rather than of the individual, and it reflected a generous amount of the philosophy of the New Deal and the welfare state. It imposed quantitative limitations on land holdings by aliens and provided against alien exploitation of natural resources, agricultural lands, and public utilities by limiting alien ownership and franchises to corporations at least 60 percent owned by Philippine citizens. The document also granted unusually strong powers to the Philippine president. He was authorized, in time of war or emergency, to promulgate any rules and regulations necessary to carry out a declared national policy.[30] It was on the basis of this authorization that President Marcos would proclaim martial law in 1972.

After the creation of the Commonwealth, both the United States and the Philippines discovered how hard it was to carry out a program for independence in the shadow of war. The United States was eager to reduce its commitments but was unwilling to sacrifice the Philippines to the appetite of Japan. It was difficult to devise a policy that would guarantee the national interests of the United States for the duration of U.S. sovereignty and at the same time provide the basis on which an independent Philippines could take care of itself in a menacing international environment.

In November 1935, the people of the Philippines elected Manuel Quezon as their first president and Sergio Osmena as their first vice-

29 U.S., *Statutes at Large,* 73rd Congress, vol. 48, part 1, pp. 456-465. For the legislative course of the independence bills through the U.S. Congress, see Grunder and Livezey, *The Philippines and the United States,* pp. 195-219.

30 U.S. Congress, *House Document, No. 400,* 74th Congress, 2nd session. This is a compilation of documents pertaining to the inauguration of the Philippine Commonwealth.

president. The Commonwealth government was officially proclaimed, which meant that independence would become automatic on July 4, 1946. Frank Murphy, the last American governor general, became the first of the new high commissioners. He was followed by Paul McNutt (1937–39) and Francis B. Sayre (1939–43), who was in office at the outbreak of World War II.

The Commonwealth government was dominated by the Nacionalista party, and the party was dominated by President Quezon. He gathered all political power in his own hands and ran the country with the flair of a Latin American *jefe,* backed by landed oligarchs, moneyed businessmen, and social aristocrats. In 1936 Quezon, much to the chagrin of his ultra-conservative backers, released Evangelista from jail and relegalized the Communist party. To alleviate the worst tensions in the Luzon rice bowl and to thwart the Socialists and Communists who were trying to capture the leadership of the dissatisfied peasants, he launched his own reform program, which he labeled "Social Justice." He pushed ahead vigorously with the purchase of estates and distribution of land and established resettlement areas in Mindanao for the depressed and crowded population of Central Luzon. Quezon took the side of small farmers against his own *cacique* supporters and thus sharpened the clash of interests between the peasant unions and landlord associations. Throughout the Commonwealth period, discontent in the rural Philippines around Manila seethed to the point of violence.[31] In 1939 Quezon engineered amendments to the constitution that changed the tenure of the president from six years to four years, with the possibility of one reelection.[32]

High Commissioner McNutt called the Philippines under the United States the one happy spot in an unhappy Orient, a spot where decency, democracy, and peace reigned and where the peculiar culture of America held forth the torch of liberty and brotherhood. He believed that if the United States should withdraw from the Philippines, it would lose its open door policy, its freedom of the seas, and its voice in Oriental diplomacy. "While our flag flies over the islands," he said, "no foreign power will trespass; if our flag comes down, the Philippines

[31] Sturtevant, "Philippine Social Structure and Agrarian Unrest," pp. 206-218. See also *Fifth Annual Report of the United States High Commissioner to the Philippine Islands to the President and Congress of the United States Covering the Fiscal Year July 1, 1940 to June 30, 1941* (Washington, D.C.: 1943), p. 34.
[32] Hayden, *The Philippines*, pp. 55-60, for an analysis of the amendments, the reasoning behind them, and the procedure by which they became part of the constitution.

will become a bloody battleground and the center of war within war for a generation."[33]

In contrast with his predecessor, High Commissioner Sayre believed that it was too late for the United States and the Philippines to pursue any course but independence as scheduled, in spite of World War II. In his heart, however, he doubted the viability of an independent Philippines because of the political, economic, and security obstacles he saw looming.[34]

With the approach of independence, economic problems became increasingly troublesome in the relations between the United States and the Philippines. Naturally, the Americans wished to protect the investments and trade of their own nationals, while the Philippines sought a complete readjustment of economic relations to promote national economic development.

The problems inherited from the American regime seemed overwhelming as they became Philippine responsibilities. Philippine agriculture could scarcely feed a fast-growing population, and the rice and corn lands were plagued with maldistribution of land, wealth, and income. The capital crops of the Philippines, mainly sugar, depended upon the American market. No prospect was in sight for industrialization because of the lack of capital and technical know-how. Domestic trade was in the hands of the ethnic Chinese in the Philippines, and foreign trade was controlled by American, Chinese, or Spanish nationals resident in the Philippines. Some Philippine government enterprises had been set up, but they were inefficiently managed and uniformly in debt. A long time would be required for such fundamental agrarian reforms as increased production, land redistribution, and crop diversification and for a well-balanced program of industrial development. In the meantime it would not be easy for the government to

[33] Radio address delivered in the United States on March 14, 1938, quoted in the *New York Times,* March 15, 1938 and in Grunder and Livezey, *The Philippines and the United States,* pp. 228 and 229. More of High Commissioner McNutt's philosophy is presented in Gerald Wheeler, "High Commissioner McNutt," an unpublished manuscript obtainable from the History Department, San Jose State University. This study was prepared for the Philippine panel at the annual meeting of the Association for Asian Studies, San Francisco, 1975.

[34] Francis B. Sayre, *Glad Adventure* (New York: Macmillan, 1957). Sayre frequently expressed these views during the year 1941 when the author served as his executive assistant.

18

remain solvent and provide financial stability. The level of revenues was modest and the demand for public expenditures[35] was growing.

Presidents Roosevelt and Quezon cooperated in the appointment of a Joint Preparatory Committee on Philippine Affairs to recommend means of adjusting the Philippine economy to independence. Acting on the recommendations of the committee, Congress passed the Tydings-Kocialkowski Act in 1939, which extended special economic relations for fifteen years after independence. American products entering the Philippines would enjoy tariff preferences through 1960, and such Philippine products as sugar, cordage, cigars, scrap and filler tobacco, coconut oil, embroideries, and shell and pearl buttons would be given special benefits in the American market for that period.[36] The scheme of diminishing duty-free quotas instead of gradually increasing tariff rates envisaged in the 1934 act was never put to the test. With the outbreak of the war in Europe in September 1939, the United States launched an effort to make the Philippines defensible regardless of cost.

President Quezon, on his part, addressed himself to the problems of Philippine security from the standpoint of the Commonwealth government. Initially, he had little faith in proposals for neutralization and undertook to raise a citizen's army comparable to that of Switzerland. With General MacArthur as his adviser and field marshal, he committed almost a quarter of his national budget to the armed forces of the Philippines. After the collapse of the small nations in Europe to Hitler, Quezon and MacArthur gave up the idea of self-reliance. Because of mounting dangers and increasing costs, it seemed futile for Filipinos to spend their money for defense. It would be up to the United States to assume full responsibility and all the costs for defense until the U.S.–Philippine tie might be completely severed.

War and Rehabilitation

Within hours after Pearl Harbor, Japanese bombs destroyed the American security position in the Philippines, but it took nearly a month for the Japanese forces to reach Manila. President Quezon accompanied High Commissioner Sayre and General MacArthur to

---

[35] Shirley Jenkins, *American Economic Policy toward the Philippines* (Stanford: Stanford University Press, 1953). No page references are given because each chapter analyzes a specific aspect of the totality of economic problems.
[36] U.S., *Statutes at Large*, 76th Congress, vol. 53, pt. 2, pp. 1226-1234.

Corregidor and took the government with him into exile. Quezon later fled to Australia and thence to Washington, where he remained as head of the legitimate Commonwealth government until his death in August 1944. He was succeeded in office by his long-time colleague, Sergio Osmena.

During the war, some Filipinos became anti-Japanese guerrillas, fleeing from the cities to join their relatives hiding in the hills. Others, like the Japanese puppet-president Jose Laurel, collaborated.[37] One effective guerrilla band, made up of agrarian discontents, patriotic peasants, Socialists, and Communists, under Luis Taruc, organized a People's Liberation Army against Japan, known locally as the Hukbalahaps or Huks for short. They conceived of themselves as part of the worldwide anti-Fascist united front and established guerrilla bases after the fashion of Mao Tse-tung throughout the mountainous regions of northern Luzon. They claimed to have killed 25,000 victims, of whom 5,000 were Japanese and the rest alleged collaborators. At the war's end the Huks had an army of 10,000 with 100,000 reserves. They were well supplied with guns and ammunition and represented the only political authority outside Manila. They were determined to extend their power by ordinary political processes if possible, by force against the government if necessary.[38]

The return of the Americans to the Philippines began with landings in Leyte and in Luzon, north of Manila. On February 13, 1945, General MacArthur recaptured Manila and within a few weeks he turned the civilian government over to President Osmena. With MacArthur absorbed in preparations for the invasion of Japan, Osmena was left to tackle the problems at home. While the American Congress pondered the best way to help the Philippines, Paul McNutt was sent back to the Philippines in December 1945 as the last high commissioner. His instructions were to investigate agrarian unrest, the status of guerrilla armies, and the influence of ex-collaborators in the Manila government as well as to ameliorate economic and financial conditions in the Philippines, dispose of surplus war materials and property con-

---

[37] U.S. High Commissioner to the Philippine Islands, *Annual Reports* for 1940, 1941, and 1942, for contemporary accounts of events. See also Teodoro Agoncillo, *Fateful Years: Japan's Adventure in the Philippines, 1941-1945*, 2 vols. (Quezon City: University of the Philippines, 1965) and David J. Steinberg, *Philippine Collaboration in World War II* (Ann Arbor: University of Michigan Press, 1967).

[38] Alvin Scaff, *The Philippine Answer to Communism* (Stanford: Stanford University Press, 1955), pp. 26-67.

fiscated from the Japanese, investigate veterans' welfare, assist in training and equipping a nonmilitary Philippine constabulary, and utilize available marine tonnage for the benefit of the Philippines.[39]

Although many parts of the country were still under the control of the American army or irregular guerrilla bands, President Osmena set April 23, 1946, as the date for national elections. The Osmena Nacionalistas were beaten at the polls by the new and more vigorous party, the Liberal Nacionalistas, led by General Manuel Roxas, who became president of the independent Republic of the Philippines on May 15, 1946.[40] The Huks joined with other opposition elements in a party known as the Democratic Alliance and were successful in winning the election of seven of their leaders, including Luis Taruc, to the Philippine Congress. A confrontation between the government and the Huks became inevitable when the duly elected Huks were expelled.[41]

Meanwhile, the United States was proceeding with plans for rehabilitation, economic assistance, and independence. The Tydings or Philippine Rehabilitation Act and the Bell or Philippine Trade Act, which became law on April 30, 1946, two months before independence, made $620 million immediately available for rehabilitation and provided for preferential trade arrangements lasting far beyond the date of independence. These acts were hailed as indications of American generosity—generosity tinged with self-interest.[42]

The sum of $620 million was disappointingly small to the Filipinos, who had been led to believe that they would receive compensation for every last chicken and water buffalo that had been lost in the war. Payments were to be made to Philippine government agencies, to Americans who had suffered losses in the Philippines, and to individual Filipino claimants. No payment in excess of $500 was to be made before the provisions of the trade act were accepted in the Philippines.

---

[39] Grunder and Livezey, *The Philippines and the United States,* p. 249. The instructions to McNutt represented a compromise of views held by Truman's advisers on how the Philippines should be treated.

[40] David Bernstein, *The Philippine Story* (New York: Farrar, Straus, 1947) and Hernando Abaya, *Betrayal of the Philippines* (New York: A. A. Wyn, 1946). These are personal accounts stressing particular Philippine points of view.

[41] Luis Taruc, *He Who Rides the Tiger* (New York: Praeger, 1967), pp. 25-26.

[42] U.S., *Statutes at Large,* 79th Congress, 2nd session, vol. 60, part 1, pp. 128-140; 141-159. For a good discussion of these acts see Grunder and Livezey, *The Philippines and the United States,* p. 250 ff.; George Taylor, *The Philippines and the United States* (New York: Praeger, 1964), p. 124 ff.; and Jenkins, *American Economic Policy,* p. 64 ff.

According to these provisions, American goods, without quota limit, were to be granted free entry into the Philippines for eight years, after which they would be subject to a gradually ascending tariff for twenty years, paying full duty by 1974. Philippine goods, subject to a generous quota limitation, were to be granted free entry into the United States likewise for eight years, after which they would be subject to either rising tariffs or declining quotas. Filipinos pointed out that the trade act benefitted not only Filipinos but also the Americans who had investment and trading interests in the Philippines. Other provisions of the trade act were accepted but were regarded by the Filipinos as clearly discriminatory. The Philippine peso was pegged to the American dollar, thus limiting the Philippines' freedom of financial action, and the immigration of Filipinos to the United States was severely restricted. The most controversial provision was the so-called parity clause:

> The disposition, exploitation, development and utilization of all agricultural, timber, and mineral lands of the public domain, the waters, minerals, coal, petroleum, and mineral resources of the Philippines, and the operation of public utilities, shall, if open to any person, be open to citizens of the United States and to all forms of business enterprise owned or controlled, directly or indirectly, by United States citizens.[43]

This clause required an amendment of the Philippine constitution which mandated 60 percent Filipino participation in public corporations. President Roxas objected to the handout of Philippine resources but he needed American help and he needed it quickly. Swallowing its national pride, the Roxas government brought about the necessary constitutional amendment and accepted the Philippine Trade Act in order to receive the benefits of the Rehabilitation Act. A pound of flesh was the price exacted for American capital.[44]

Independence, 1946–1965

In the midst of difficult circumstances, both the United States and the Republic of the Philippines addressed themselves to the problems of

[43] Quoted in Grunder and Livezey, *The Philippines and the United States*, p. 62. U.S. Department of State Press Release no. 914, December 18, 1946, announced the U.S.-Philippine agreement based on the Philippine Trade Act.

[44] It should be pointed out that the required amendment would not have passed the Philippine Congress had it not been for the expulsion of the seven Huks, who were naturally anticapitalist and opposed to the trade act.

their new relationship. Two nations, unequal in strength and experience, would have to learn to pursue their distinctive goals on the basis of equality and mutual respect. The real threat to Philippine security— badly underrated in the United States—was domestic political chaos stemming from the weakness of the national government and the magnitude of civil revolt. It was assumed in Washington that the government of the Philippines was impregnable because it was democratic in form and American in inspiration. A two-party system, complete with national elections and a representative government, seemed to be operating satisfactorily. Washington did not fully comprehend the extent to which political patterns familiar in the United States would be twisted and strained in an alien environment by such traditional Filipino social concepts as *pakikisama,* the spirit of camaraderie, and *utang na loob,* the code of interpersonal obligations.

The Filipinization of American democracy produced a precarious and highly unstable government. The two parties, Nacionalista and Liberal, had risen to prominence on the single issue of independence— and both lacked a clear-cut philosophy or blueprint for political operation. Party organization was brittle and fluctuating. A candidate rejected by one party could easily shift to the other. National elections were won by promises or favors and violence and corruption soon came to characterize Philippine politics. The president and Congress could hardly function according to the principle of checks and balances since both were representative of the same economic and social strata in Philippine society.

The national government was too weak to cope with internal dissension, which was spreading rapidly. The Huks virtually declared war on the establishment and were outlawed by President Roxas. Defiant, they exercised de facto political control over the hinterland of Luzon and the highways that led to Manila. They espoused Communist principles, chose Communist leaders, and called for the overthrow of imperialists, feudal landlords, and business *compradores.* Creating a reign of terror in the countryside, they threatened to overthrow the national government. All of Luzon outside Manila itself was Huk territory. Massive help from the United States was needed if Philippine national security were to be protected.

The Philippines needed American help for economic reasons as well. Filipinos who had lost everything in the war saw the Americans as their only hope. With the return of peace, Philippine farmers

23

planted sufficient crops to keep the nation from starving, but foreign capital was needed to get the economy moving. Surplus property from the United States was welcomed, as were back pay for veterans and guerrillas, U.S. loans, and the transfer of substantial operating funds from Washington to Manila. Yet American aid was arriving too slowly to satisfy the impatient Filipinos. They resented the slow progress of the Tydings rehabilitation and Bell trade bills through the legislative mill in Washington and extended open arms to American old-timers and new investors who came to the Philippines with money and energy to help get the economy going. The parity clause, though it had sown the seeds of ill will between the two nations, seemed to be a reasonable price for the infusion of new financial blood.

President Roxas, 1946–1948. Manuel Roxas, president of the Philippines when independence was granted, was a thoroughgoing capitalist schooled in the politics of Quezonian nationalism. He was totally committed to cooperation with the United States as the only hope for a prosperous future for the Philippines. He therefore welcomed all the economic assistance he could obtain from the United States and concluded agreements on military bases and the military assistance program with the Americans.[45] He had no doubts about linking the security of the Philippines to American power in the Western Pacific.

Although President Roxas first treated the Huks as ordinary dissidents, he came to the view that they and their propaganda arm, the National Peasants' Union, should be outlawed as foreign-supported Communist agents. He pointed out that the Huks were antigovernment and blatantly anti-American, demanding abrogation of the American trade agreement, amelioration of the plight of the populace struggling in the clutches of American imperialists, and an end to the mock independence that had been obtained from the United States. They urged the recall of American military forces from the Philippines and openly advocated the linking of their program with those of insurgents in Malaya, Burma, Vietnam, and China.

This identification of the Huks with Communist insurgency throughout the world tended to throw the governments of the United

---

[45] Department of Foreign Affairs Treaty Series, vol. 1, *Agreement between the Republic of the Philippines and the United States of America Concerning Military Bases* (Manila: Government of the Philippines, 1948), pp. 144-160. See also Department of State Press Release, March 14, 1947 for agreement concerning military bases and March 21, 1947 for agreement providing for military assistance.

24

States and the Philippines closer together. The commitment to the anti-Communist side in the cold war was as complete in Manila as it was in Washington. The perception of the Huks as a part of a world-wide Communist conspiracy was a major factor in prompting the Philippines to seek military and economic aid from the United States, and in persuading the United States to grant it. Both sides tended to overlook the seriousness of the domestic conditions that had led to agrarian unrest in the first place. The attitude of the Philippine government toward international communism caused the Soviet leaders to lump together the Filipinos, Nationalist Chinese, and South Koreans as the American lackeys in Asia.[46]

In foreign policy President Roxas did not blindly follow the American lead; some of the measures he adopted showed a true spirit of independence. He recognized that the protection of Philippine interests would on occasion demand action distinct from and opposed to the interests of the United States. His goverment resented the budding love affair between Japan and the forces of the American occupation. With his nation still suffering from the ravages of war, he felt the United States was moving too far and too fast toward reconciliation. He wanted harsh treatment for Japanese war criminals and advance reparations payments from Japan pending a formal treaty of peace.

The Roxas administration concluded a treaty of friendship with Nationalist China (then at Nanking but later at Taipei) defining reciprocal rights of travel, residence, property, and occupation as well as diplomatic immunities and consular privileges. The net effect of this treaty was that Chiang Kai-shek, not Mao Tse-tung, would have the right to look after the interests of the Chinese in the Philippines in matters of immigration, trade and travel, naturalization, and protection of personal and property rights.[47]

On the last day of his life, April 15, 1948, President Roxas delivered an address at Clark Field which showed the depth of his commitment to the philosophy and the cause of the United States.

---

[46] Luis Taruc, *Born of the People* (New York: International Publishers, 1953), Alvin H. Scaff, *The Philippine Answer to Communism*, and Milton W. Meyer, *Diplomatic History of the Philippine Republic* (Honolulu: University of Hawaii Press, 1965) give contrasting views of the nature and extent of the Huk menace to Philippine security.

[47] Republic of the Philippines, *Official Gazette*, vol. 43, section 6 (June 1947), pp. 2281-2283 for text of treaty; see also Republic of the Philippines, *Congressional Record*, 1st Congress, 2nd session, Senate, vol. 2, section 38 (April 22, 1947), pp. 378-579.

Just before he was stricken with a fatal heart attack, he said that if war should come, a new war waged by aggressor nations against the forces of freedom and liberty—he was certain that American and Philippine soldiers would again fight side by side in the same trenches or in the air in defense of justice, freedom, and other principles that both nations cherished.

President Quirino, 1948–1953. Vice-President Quirino, who succeeded Roxas to the presidency, followed closely the political and diplomatic lead of his predecessor in the early phase of his administration. He promised unconditional solidarity with the United States, which he thought of as his nation's best friend. Shortly after his succession to office, he visited Washington and expounded his view of Philippine-American relations in an address to the United States Senate. He said:

> Today the Republic of the Philippines stands as a monument to the great American dream of freedom, a vital outpost of freedom and democracy on our side of the world. . . . The Filipino people have found in the democracy you have implanted in our land the fullness of life and enjoyment of its blessings, and they will not surrender them in exchange for the false utopian promises of any utilitarian system. . . .
>
> Our most urgent problem is security, lying as we do athwart the advancing tide of communism. Asia is bound to be lost to communism unless something of the courage and vision that went into the forging of the democratic defenses in Europe is applied to the forging of a similar system of defense in Asia. . . . Only the blind will say that the menace to the Philippines does not menace America, for even the great democracy of America cannot remain unconcerned wherever and whenever the survival of free men in a free world is at stake.[48]

American war damage payments were substantially concluded during the Quirino administration and negotiations were initiated for a new trade agreement. The Filipinos brought pressure for ever-increasing military and economic assistance as their internal difficulties multiplied. They talked a great deal more of American obligations than of American generosity.

In response to a request from President Quirino, President Truman sent an Economic Survey Mission, headed by Daniel W. Bell, former undersecretary of the treasury, to make a further diagnosis of the ills

---

48 Embassy of the Republic of the Philippines, "Address of President Quirino to United States Senate," Washington, D.C., August 9, 1949.

of the Philippines and to prescribe appropriate remedies. After a thoroughgoing study of agriculture, industry, trade, and taxation, the mission concluded that the basic economic problems of the Philippines could be solved only by a determined effort on the part of the Philippine government and people, with the aid of the United States, to increase production and improve productive efficiency, raise the level of wages and farm income, and open new opportunities for work and acquiring land. In addition, the mission recommended that reforms be implemented in every phase of Philippine government operation, stressing the need to eliminate graft and corruption. If the Philippines would do its part, the United States would continue its military assistance to the Philippines and would make available $250 million in ten years for economic aid.[49]

The Bell report reminded the Philippines as gently as possible of the shortcomings of its government, but it stirred up a new kind of response to the United States. An end to the love feast was indicated by an official on the staff of President Quirino who wrote in a newspaper commentary:

> We are pikers compared to the graft and corruption of our American mentors. . . . We are not rich enough to cover up our own stink and be lofty and moral about it before a devastated and hungry world. . . . Americans do not have a corner on all the stock there is of efficiency, competence, vision and integrity in the world.[50]

Criticisms of the United States were heard more frequently in the Philippines. Some Filipinos believed the satellite economic relationship between the Philippines and the United States was as humiliating as the prewar relationship had been. The Americans were accused of granting economic aid for their own selfish purposes and using military assistance as a device for getting rid of old, deteriorated arms, battle worn and inadequate even to cope with Philippine internal disorder.[51]

It was Manila's nightmare that the United States might go too far in supporting postwar Japan's ambition to become the workshop of

---

[49] U.S. Department of State, Publication 4010, Far East Series, No. 38, *Report to the President of the United States by the Economic Mission to the Philippines* (Washington, D.C.: 1950).

[50] *Manila Chronicle*, October 26, 1950. Extensively quoted in Taylor, *The Philippines and the U.S.*, pp. 140-141.

[51] *New York Times*, February 10, 1950. This particular accusation was attributed to Camilio Osias, the minority leader in the Philippine Senate.

Asia. The Philippines did not believe that Japan could be transformed from an aggressive, feudalistic, militaristic police state into a practicing democracy in a few short years. President Quirino was among the first to recognize the importance of Japan as an ally in the fight against communism in Asia and as a vital element in the achievement of international stability in the Far East. Nevertheless, he could not rid himself entirely of the fear that the United States in backing Japan would condemn the Philippines to becoming a nation of slaves worshipping at the temple of the Japanese goddess Amaterasu Omikami and paying obeisance to the emperor of Japan.[52]

President Quirino wanted some kind of Pacific pact, or an international arrangement corresponding to NATO in Europe. As early as January 1949, when the Asian nations met in New Delhi to discuss the problem of the Dutch in Indonesia, the Philippine delegate was instructed to sound out his colleagues on the possibility of a permanent organization of all Asian nations, regardless of ideology, for economic, political, cultural, and military cooperation. But Quirino's proposal was received with indifference.[53]

Subsequently President Quirino tried a new approach for a Pacific pact. He suggested the founding of a limited organization consisting of non-Communists who might form a third force to oppose Communist expansion with the backing of the United States. That was before the Korean War, when the United States welcomed opposition to Communist expansion but shied away from military commitment. As the Korean situation deteriorated, however, President Quirino was encouraged to continue his efforts to form an organization for the preservation of the democratic way of life. In May 1950 he convened a conference in Baguio, a mountain resort in the Philippines, attended by Australia, Pakistan, India, Ceylon, Thailand, and Indonesia. Chiang Kai-shek was not invited, nor was Syngman Rhee or any representative from the beleaguered states of Indochina. The conference adopted a single resolution recommending cultural, commercial, and financial cooperation, but nothing was said of political or military cooperation against communism.

---

52 Townsend Hoopes, *The Devil and John Foster Dulles* (Boston: Little, Brown, 1973), p. 106. Hoopes bases this passage on his interview with John Allison, who was assistant to Dulles in negotiating the Japanese peace treaty.

53 Meyer, *Diplomatic History of the Philippines*, Chapter 7, "Search for a Pacific Pact" is a well-documented analysis of President Quirino's efforts to achieve a Pacific pact.

The Philippines, before the outbreak of the fighting in Korea on June 25, 1950, weighed the possibilities of neutralism—that is, non-alignment—which would allow it a free hand in dealing with the United States, the U.S.S.R., or the newly emerged People's Republic of China, established on October 1, 1949. Three days before the attack on South Korea, the Philippine secretary of foreign affairs was still asking the United States to recognize the validity of neutralism and to accept the fact that democracy might not work everywhere in Asia. Not all nationalist movements, he urged, should be branded as Communist.

This position was abandoned when war actually came to Korea. President Quirino deserted his old stand on an all-Asian non-ideological organization and lined up on the American side. His speeches became passionately anti-Communist and he sent Philippine troops to fight with the United Nations force in Korea. This change in policy aroused the stiff opposition of some Nacionalistas, notably Senator Claro Recto, who wished to preserve the former policy of independent action and to avoid unequivocal allegiance to American leadership in the cold war.

In 1951 President Quirino accepted the Treaty of Peace with Japan and signed the Mutual Defense Treaty with the United States.[54] The Mutual Defense Treaty promised that in the event of an attack on the Philippines, the United States would act to meet the common dangers in accordance with its constitutional processes, but it contained no provision for automatic assistance. Recto argued that the commitment in the Mutual Defense Treaty was vague and amounted to no commitment at all. He wanted the Philippines to have the benefit of the NATO formula, stipulating that an armed attack against either of the contracting parties in the Pacific area should be considered as an attack against both and that in the event of such an armed attack against the Philippines, the United States would assist the Philippines by taking immediate action to repel the attack and to restore and maintain the security of the Philippines and of the Pacific area. Because of the unwillingness of the Americans to accept such an obligation, Recto had profound misgivings about the quality and the permanence of the American commitment to Asia.

Recto made it clear that in the event of war between the United States and the Soviet Union, the Filipinos would be on the side of

---

[54] Republic of the Philippines, Department of Foreign Affairs, *Mutual Defense Treaty, 1951, between the Republic of the Philippines and the United States of America*, Treaty Series, vol. 2, Manila, January 1953, p. 14.

the American people, but he disliked the idea that the Philippines had elected to disregard all the dictates of prudence and national security. He stated his case emphatically: In the world parliament of the United Nations, it is no more difficult to predict that the Philippines will vote with the American Union than that the Ukraine will vote with the Soviet Union. . . . We have a mendicant foreign policy, and as beggars we cannot be choosers; we can safely be ignored, taken for granted, dictated to, made to wait at the door, hat in hand, to go in only when invited. . . . Dependent entirely on American arms, we find it increasingly difficult to procure them; having rested our hopes on American bases, we find them unmanned, dismantled and in the great majority abandoned, so that rather than sources of protection they may become targets for attack.[55]

In reply to Recto, Secretary of Foreign Affairs Romulo Carlos denied that the government was mendicant or subservient and that the phrase "independent foreign policy" had any meaning. Romulo argued that full cooperation with the United States was the only way to protect the Philippine national interest or even to survive. "We as pigmies cannot step aside while giants fight," he said.

> The United States giant does not menace us, the Soviet Union and China do, and the American giant is the only protection we have from communist giants. . . . We are on the communist time table, we want our place to be with dignity and courage among the legions of the free. The instinct to be free cannot be quenched by the anxiety to be safe.[56]

Romulo believed that the Mutual Defense Treaty, as signed, was adequate for the Philippines despite the absence of a provision for automatic assistance. The United States, Romulo said, did not intend to abandon Asia and would from its own self-interest come to the aid of the Philippines. In this sentiment, he was supported by Ramon Magsaysay, the Philippine secretary of national defense. Both men felt that the Mutual Defense Treaty amounted to a clearcut military alliance between two sovereign nations and that, together with the American military bases in the Philippines, it gave positive evidence that the

---

[55] Claro M. Recto, *Commencement Address*, University of the Philippines, delivered April 17, 1951, printed and circulated by the University of the Philippines, Quezon City.

[56] Carlos P. Romulo, *Commencement Address*, University of the East, delivered April 28, 1951, printed and circulated by the University of the Philippines, Manila.

United States was willing to do whatever was necessary to protect the Philippines.

The cooperation between the United States and the Philippines, revitalized after the outbreak of hostilities in Korea, began to pay handsome dividends in the field of internal security. In 1950 when President Quirino proved unequal to the task of putting down the Huk insurgents by his own policies, he gave Magsaysay practically a free hand in restoring law and order. Magsaysay injected a driving spirit into the campaign against the Huks and forced his soldiers to become friends with the people. He struck at the insurgents and, more important, at the roots of insurgency. He not only fought the Huks, he offered land and a new life to those who would surrender. For the moment, he seemed to have broken the back of the rebel movement.

With a generous amount of American assistance and advice, Magsaysay purged the army of its worst leaders and reorganized the Department of Defense. To the dismay of the party in power, he used the revitalized army to clean up the election process, and in so doing, Magsaysay, the man of the masses, became a national hero. He sought the presidency of his country in order to complete his work. Breaking with Quirino and the Liberals, he joined with Senator Recto and the former collaborator Jose Laurel in the Nacionalista party. In 1953, as Nacionalista nominee for the presidency, Magsaysay took his campaign to the slums and to the poor in the countryside and won a landslide victory.

President Magsaysay, 1953–1957. At the time of his election, Magsaysay was well and favorably known in the United States as a pro-American. His guerrilla record had been highly publicized, and he had spent much of his term as a Philippine congressman (1946–1950) in the United States, a one-man lobby for the Philippine veterans and the Philippine army. Magsaysay had argued that every penny spent on the Philippine veterans was an investment in American security and Philippine good will. His integrity and sincerity had attracted the support of many influential Americans in Washington and New York. At the tomb of the unknown soldier in Arlington, Magsaysay placed a wreath that bore the inscription, "To the unknown soldier, who gave his life for ideals stronger than death, from his Filipino comrade." In the Congress of the Philippines, he became chairman of the Committee on National Defense and the eloquent champion of Philippine-American cooperation in the struggle against communism.[57]

The *New York Times* praised Magsaysay as a leader of integrity, imagination, courage, and simplicity, and the *Herald Tribune* described him as an eminent figure, a bulwark against Communist aggression, a pillar of democratic government, and an extraordinarily vivid and commanding personality. Admiral Raymond Spruance, U.S. ambassador to the Philippines, and General Albert Pierson, chief of the Joint U.S. Military Advisory Group (JUSMAG) in Manila quietly boosted the Magsaysay stock.[58] Magsaysay made no secret of his pro-American sentiments. During his campaign for the presidency, he himself said, after listening to the "Star Spangled Banner,"

> I heard it last when I was in the hills in the latter part of July, 1942. That song means a lot to me and the Filipino people. . . . I know now the Republic of the Philippines is America's baby. We're in the same family. I was not so sure in 1946, after we were given our independence, that American-Philippine unity would last undiminshed. These doubts are gone. We belong together and know it.[59]

As president, Magsaysay gave priority to domestic policies safeguarding national security, promoting the well-being of the masses, accelerating the country's economic development, and improving the standards of public service. His effectiveness lay not so much in what he said as in the way he said it. He chose the right words, made them intelligible to the humble people in the villages, and gave the peasants the feeling that somebody cared. He told his people, "barefeet will always be welcomed in the president's palace." [60]

Magsaysay's faith in the rightness of the policies of the United States never wavered. He was as adamant as Secretary of State John Foster Dulles in his belief that communism was an unremitting campaign

---

[57] José Velaso Abueva, *Ramon Magsaysay: A Political Biography* (Manila: Solidaridad Publishing House, 1971), pp. 124, 126, and 214n.

[58] For two interesting views of Magsaysay given by his American supporters, see Thomas B. Buell, *Quiet Warrior, a Biography of Admiral Raymond A. Spruance* (Boston: Little, Brown, 1974), particularly Chapter 25, which contains a vivid description of the work of the CIA during the time of the Magsaysay election, and Edward Geary Lansdale, *In the Midst of Wars, an American's Mission to Southeast Asia* (New York: Harper and Row, 1972), particularly Chapter 3, pp. 32-60.

[59] Abueva, *Magsaysay*, p. 214 n.

[60] Agnes Newton Keith, *Barefeet in the Palace* (Boston: Little, Brown, 1955). A perceptive, popular account of Magsaysay and his relationship with the people.

to rule the earth, to eradicate individual liberty, to destroy God and the souls of men.[61] He charged that the leaders of international communism were seeking by every means—open aggression, subversion, indirect support of armed insurrection—to advance their ambitions in Southeast Asia and that they intended to take over free countries by force if necessary.

Magsaysay rejected the idea that communism was the wave of the future. To him, world freedom was destined to overcome, thanks to the genius and God-given resources of America. He suggested that if there were still those who suspected American motives, knowledge of the Philippine-American experience would help to change their attitude. The original, the true spirit of America would always dominate American relations not only with the Philippines but with all free nations, he was convinced. For the free world, which depended so much on the United States for strength, that true spirit of America was the best guarantee of understanding, security, and freedom.

In 1954 Magsaysay acted as host to the meeting that produced the Southeast Asia Collective Defense Treaty, more commonly called the Manila Pact, which was signed by the Philippines, Thailand, Pakistan, France, Australia, New Zealand, the United Kingdom, and the United States, who joined in a Southeast Asia Treaty Organization (SEATO) designed primarily to prevent armed Communist aggression in Southeast Asia immediately after the defeat of France in Indochina. By this treaty, it was agreed that, in the event of aggression by means of armed attack in the treaty area against any of the parties, the signatories would act to meet the common danger in accordance with their constitutional processes and that they would consult together to agree on measures for common defense if any one of them considered the inviolability, territorial integrity, sovereignty, or political independence of any party to the treaty threatened other than by armed attack. Furthermore, Magsaysay refused to recognize Communist China and opposed the entry of Peking into the United Nations. On February 3, 1955, he placed the Philippines squarely behind the United States in the offshore islands controversy. He did not want the United States to change its China policy in any way, and he thought that an understanding with Chiang Kai-shek would be useful to him in dealing with the powerful Chinese ethnic minority in the Philippines.

[61] Ramon Magsaysay, "Roots of Philippine Policy," in *Foreign Affairs* (New York: Council on Foreign Relations, 1956), vol. 35, no. 1, pp. 29-36. See also Abueva, *Magsaysay*, p. 448 ff.

Magsaysay supported the Diem regime in South Vietnam and backed the policies of the United States in Indochina, whatever their ambiguities and vacillations, referring repeatedly to the United States as his first line of defense against insurgency and possible aggression from the Asian mainland. He regarded Philippine relations with the United States as analogous to friendship between individuals: since America was powerful and affluent it could be counted on to protect the weak and the poor. Unabashedly trusting the United States throughout his administration, Magsaysay counted many Americans among his closest personal friends and ignored his opponents' charge that he was disgustingly pro-American.[62]

Nor did Magsaysay shy away from quarrels with the United States as they occurred. He was the first to undertake negotiations with the Americans on the problems stemming from the U.S. bases in the Philippines. Occasional incidents involving American military personnel and Philippine civilians aroused bad feelings in Olongapo, near the Subic Bay naval base, and in Angeles City, near Clark Field. Some Filipinos wanted Magsaysay to repeal the Military Bases Agreement of 1947, but he refused, preferring to work out an understanding on each issue as it arose. The precedent he established was followed by succeeding administrations. Magsaysay pressed for affirmation of Philippine rights to mineral resources on base lands and he obtained from visiting Vice-President Nixon a formal statement acknowledging Philippine sovereignty over the bases. He also began the long series of discussions looking to sharper definition of respective U.S.-Philippine rights of jurisdiction over off-duty, off-base offenses.[63]

In economic controversies, President Magsaysay strenuously defended the Philippine position. He wanted more generous treatment for Filipino employees of American firms and for Filipino laborers on Guam. He objected to excessive imports of Virginia leaf tobacco into the Philippines and pushed for larger quotas for Philippine sugar entering the United States duty-free. The United States did too much for Japan and not enough for the Philippines, he complained. He also alleged that the United States used the aid program to keep the Philippines in economic bondage and pressed for the recognition of almost $1 billion worth of Philippine claims against the United States.

---

[62] Abueva, *Magsaysay*, p. 389.
[63] Ibid., pp. 339 ff. and 462-468.

Magsaysay authorized the negotiation of the Laurel-Langley trade agreement, which became effective in 1956 and which put an end to the most galling features of the existing trade patterns by prescribing conditions for special economic relations that would last until July 4, 1974. In this agreement, the Republic of the Philippines was given a good deal, but it was far from satisfied. The Philippines would have liked even more favorable treatment for such products as sugar and cigars in the American market and complained of shabby treatment by its powerful trading partner. One Philippine congressman went so far as to say that as a result of American short-sightedness, the prevailing attitude toward the United States in the Philippines might well change from admiration and hero worship to disillusionment and hostility.[64]

On May 9, 1956, the Philippines and Japan signed a reparations agreement, which provided that Japan should pay $550 million in indemnities and advance $250 million in credits over the next twenty years for economic development in the Philippines. The Japanese were to assist in almost every type of economic activity including shipping, industrialization, development of mineral and forest reserves, improvement of railways, port facilities, highways, rural roads, communications, land utilization, irrigation systems, and reconstruction of schools, churches, and hospitals. This agreement brought millions of dollars to the Philippines—to individuals, private firms, and the government—but it caused widespread fear that Japan would gain an ominous influence in vital areas of Filipino life.[65]

During the Magsaysay administration, the first evidence of ultra-nationalism appeared. Unsympathetic, Magsaysay discouraged an extremist group that was trumpeting the slogan "Filipino First" in its campaign for increasing the Filipino share in the political and economic life of the nation. Magsaysay himself disavowed fanatics who sought to revive dead issues and cut their own people off from the outside world by a wall of suspicion, distrust, and hatred. The first targets of the ultranationalists were the ethnic Chinese, many of whom were stateless or naturalized Filipinos. The Chinese made up 2 percent of the

---

[64] For the Laurel-Langley Agreement, see the *Congressional Record*, vol. 100, part 7, June 23, 1954, pp. 8766-9767. *The American Chamber of Commerce Journal*, A. V. H. Hartendorp, ed., Manila, September 1955, p. 375, also printed the "Executive Agreement on Revised Philippine-American Trade Relations, Signed September 7." The congressman quoted was Pedro Lopez, who was killed in the plane crash that took the life of Magsaysay. See Taylor, *The Philippines and the United States*, pp. 209-210.

[65] Abueva, *Magsaysay*, pp. 401-407 and 468 ff.

population but controlled three-quarters of the commercial investment, two-thirds of the domestic trade, and one-third of the foreign trade of the Philippines. Most of the Chinese tried to keep out of politics of all sorts but obviously felt much more sympathy toward Chiang Kai-shek than toward Mao Tse-tung. In 1954, the Philippine Congress put on the books the Retail Nationalization Law, which provided that "no person who is not a citizen of the Philippines, and no association, partnership or corporation the capital of which is not wholly owned by citizens of the Philippines, shall engage directly or indirectly in the retail business."[66] While aimed primarily at the Chinese, the law was a danger signal for the Americans.

The issue of ultranationalism, which was readily equated with anti-Americanism, became the chief bone of contention between those who subscribed to the fierce spirit of independence displayed by Senator Recto and those who, like President Magsaysay and Secretary of Foreign Affairs Carlos Romulo, argued that there was no fundamental conflict between their own devotion to the Philippines and their belief that the national security and economic development were best promoted by understanding and cooperation with the United States. During the Magsaysay presidency, there appeared to be no diminution whatever in popular Filipino good will toward the United States, but journalists, columnists, and political orators began to attract a certain measure of prominence by hurling charges of anti-Americanism or pro-Americanism at one another. Magsaysay said he was quite prepared to take on any opponent on the issue of pro-Americanism in his campaign for reelection, when a plane crash ended his life on March 17, 1957.

President Garcia, 1957–1961. The death of Magsaysay so close to election time in 1957 left the Nacionalista party in disarray. Carlos P. Garcia, who as vice-president had succeeded to the presidency, teamed with José P. Laurel, Jr., on the Nacionalista ticket, while the Liberals nominated José Yulo for president, and a young lawyer, Diosdado Macapagal for vice-president. The voters split their ballots and elected Garcia president and the opposition candidate, Macapagal, vice-president.

Garcia was overwhelmed by the internal problems of the Philippines. He could not find a formula to make the government operate

---

[66] Retail Trade Nationalization Law, Republic Act 1180, 1954. See Abueva, *Magsaysay*, p. 432.

smoothly, get economic development moving, and eliminate social unrest in the countryside. With the loss of the levelheaded Magsaysay, the administration came increasingly under the influence of more extreme nationalists. Politicians in and out of Congress, teachers and students in the universities, columnists and commentators, ambitious native businessmen and left-wing agitators fanned the flames of Philippine chauvinism—and anti-Americanism. History was reinterpreted to blame the colonial heritage for all the ills of the Philippines. According to the revisionist interpretation, the Americans during their regime had been insensitive to the feelings of Asians and this had made the subject Filipinos dishonest and evasive. The new nationalists called for cutting all vestiges of Americanism, ending the colonial mentality and asserting their unique Filipino identity.

When, in 1957, Secretary Dulles told a congressional committee that the purpose of the State Department was to look after the interests of the United States and that he did not care whether or not he made friends, his critics in the Philippines had a field day. They felt that all American officials were too near-sighted to appreciate the nationalistic aspirations and cultural pride of the Filipinos. Ernesto Granada wrote that Dulles was worthy of praise for his candor, but he was an old fool if he believed that by ignoring the self-respect of other nations he could win them or keep them as reliable allies.

Many Filipinos spoke out against the United States with a bluntness that shocked their American friends. José P. Laurel, Jr., the speaker of the Philippine House of Representatives said:

> It is claimed in platitudes now tired and empty, that as the prodigious child of American enlightenment we are the living example in Asia of democracy in action. Nonsense. We are under the heel of a new oppression that shatters not our bodies but our illusions and subjects us to a great disenchantment because it takes the form of discrimination, prejudice and ingratitude, and comes with a profession of friendship.[67]

Senator Recto himself was among those who continually lambasted the new American imperialists who milked the Filipinos in their own crafty way and such brilliant columnists as Carmen Guerrero-Nakpil and I. P. Soliongco poured forth a steady stream of invective against undiminished American arrogance and racism. In a classroom

---

[67] Representative José P. Laurel, Jr., speaking in 1956. For more details on the prevalent "anti-Americanism" at that time see Claude A. Buss, *Arc of Crisis* (New York: Doubleday, 1961), especially Chapters 6 and 7.

one day, a college student remarked, "American blood has done nothing for us but increase the height of our basketball players and improve the figures of our movie stars."[68]

In keeping with the new spirit of Filipino First, the National Economic Council under the chairmanship of former Senator Dr. José Locsin, passed a resolution in 1958 to encourage Filipinos to engage in vital enterprises and industries so as to increase their share of total national economic activity. Dr. Locsin felt that it was the God-given patrimony of Filipinos to utilize and develop their own resources and he was determined to avoid a condition where Filipinos would be beggars in their own homes. A series of laws and regulations expanded the area of government ownership and planning, and gave Filipinos a more significant role in economic development. The climate for foreign investments became more oppressive. At the same time, whether because of Philippine legislation or the general improvement in world economic conditions, Philippine income and production figures showed a marked improvement. Financial reserves strengthened and the international balance of trade was favorable. Filipinos began to invest in new enterprises and to buy out many of the long-established American firms. The prospect that foreign investments in the Philippines would diminish did not seem to worry Filipinos who with self-confidence set out to show the world that they were as capable businessmen as the Americans, the Chinese or the Japanese.[69]

While anti-Americanism flourished in popular sentiment and in ultranationalistic legislation, President Garcia labored to keep official Philippine-American relations on a correct and friendly basis. On a visit to Washington in 1958, he received an assurance of support and assistance from President Eisenhower and was invited to address the Congress of the United States. Garcia eloquently renewed his vow "to stand by the United States as long as her leadership of the Free World continues to be so nobly dedicated to the supreme cause of world freedom and peace."[70] He told the Congress that the Philippines wished

---

[68] The files of the *Manila Chronicle*, illustrate the almost daily satirical criticisms of American policy. Sometimes the columns seemed vicious but more often they were cynical or merely clever. The remark here quoted was made, half in jest, during one of the author's classes at the University of the Philippines.

[69] National Economic Council, "Filipino First Policy," Resolution No. 204, August 21, 1958. For more extended treatment of the anti-American atmosphere of the time, see Buss, *Arc of Crisis*, p. 131 ff.

[70] *New York Times*, June 19, 1958. Text of the address of President Garcia to the joint session of Congress the preceding day.

to establish in Asia the validity of its claim that the product of fifty years of Philippine-American collaboration was a democracy that offered its people the reality of a free and abundant life, and he expressed determination to prove that democracy, not communism, was the answer to the spiritual and material wants of a billion Asians.

Garcia appealed for the economic assistance and foreign capital that were essential in the unending work of nation-building. Then he presented the United States with a bill drawn up during the Magsaysay administration for $800 million which he argued was due the Philippines for refunds on sugar and coconut-oil processing taxes, duties evaded, accounting errors, additional back pay for guerrillas, and allowances for Filipino veterans. The visit of Garcia to Washington, coming as it did after the launching of Sputnik and on the eve of crises in Cuba and the offshore islands, marked a low point in Philippine-American understanding.

These tensions notwithstanding, President Garcia remained fairly close to the United States in the general lines of his diplomacy. He continued to receive Japanese reparations payments, despite horrendous scandals and charges of corruption, and he signed (though the Philippines did not ratify it) a treaty of amity, commerce, and navigation with Japan. The Philippines became the mainstay of SEATO and, with Thailand and Malaya, pioneered an Association of Southeast Asia (ASA) for closer cultural and economic cooperation between themselves. The long shadow of Vietnam failed to reach the Philippines in the Garcia administration. Senator Recto called for recognition of the People's Republic of China and its entry into the United Nations, but Garcia continued to follow the lead of the United States in China policy.

Like Magsaysay, Garcia felt that good will toward the United States was still a more potent political force in the Philippines than anti-Americanism. He invited President Eisenhower to visit the Philippines in June 1960 and assured his guest that the upsurge of nationalism could not dissolve or weaken the ties of friendship that had bound the United States and the Philippines so closely together for fifty years. Good will was on the rise, and anti-Americanism on the decline when the Nacionalista Garcia lost the election of 1961 to his former vice-president, Diosdado Macapagal.

President Macapagal, 1961–1965. In the campaign of 1961, Macapagal was supported by his chief rival within the Liberal party, Senator Ferdinand E. Marcos, as part of an agreement that Macapagal,

39

rather than seeking reelection, would support Marcos for president four years later. The outcome of the election of 1961 was a foregone conclusion. The single issue, more important than nationalism or foreign affairs, was graft and corruption. The Liberal candidates accused Garcia and his "fellow-crooks" of stealing from the government and the people everything except the curtains at the windows of the president's palace.

Once in power, the Liberals launched a successful campaign against the excesses of nationalism. They criticized the Filipino First movement as sheer greed and hypocrisy and charged the Nacionalistas with using the rabble-rousing slogans of nationalism as a smoke screen for their own selfish schemes. The Liberals called the Nacionalistas patrioteers, or racketeers of patriotism, alleging that the professional nationalists looked out only for themselves and not for the welfare of the masses. The Liberals said that the Nacionalistas passed nationalistic laws only to break them, vilified foreign firms while scrambling to get jobs as legal retainers, and lived like rajahs in their air-conditioned mansions, enjoying expensive swimming pools, flashy Cadillacs, and sparkling jewels while the masses lived in want.

According to the Liberals, true nationalism should not be a partisan issue or a cloak for the selfish ambitions of an individual or a particular ethnic group. It should go beyond antiforeignism or anti-Americanism to become a positive, constructive force for all the people of the Philippines, rich and poor, Chinese, Moslem, and Filipino, working together for the common good. One of the most intelligent thinkers about nationalism, Teodoro Locsin, wrote:

> In the barrios they do not understand a thing about nationalism. If nationalism would give the people in the barrios clothes, decent homes, adequate education, larger incomes and a higher standard of living, then I would be all for it. But I have no use for those who keep saying they are nationalists but will not do a thing to help our masses live better. I am all for a positive, healthy nationalism which criticizes itself and recognizes our faults. We must broaden our horizons and not retreat into the distant past. We should sink our roots deep into the land of our fathers but let the branches of our cultural tree seek light and sustenance wherever in the world they can be found.[71]

In foreign policy, President Macapagal and his vice-president, Emmanuel Pelaez, were pledged to a program of strengthening their

---

[71] *Philippines Free Press*, January 30, 1965.

40

ties with the free world, supporting the United Nations, and increasing their influence in Asia. The Macapagal administration refused to disturb the practical stalemate with Japan and would not tolerate any changes in Philippine relations with Communists anywhere, particularly China. It turned down Russian overtures for cultural exchanges and denied visas for a touring Yugoslav basketball team. It would not allow Filipinos to travel to mainland China or Chinese Communists to enter the Philippines. In 1964 Philippine policy toward the People's Republic of China was severely shaken by the shock waves caused by China's first atomic explosion. [72]

President Macapagal anchored his foreign policy in good relations with the United States. Feeling secure in the mutual defense relationship, he was primarily concerned to maximize American assistance in solving his economic problems. In his quest for help, he did everything in his power to tone down the residual excesses of ultra-nationalism. Without the United States, he saw no way out of his domestic difficulties. The rate of population growth, near the highest in Asia, exceeded the increase in the GNP. The government's budgetary deficit together with the paucity of private savings and foreign investments left little hope for success in schemes for national development, while a Land Reform Act passed in 1963, aimed at the abolition of tenancy and share cropping, remained a dead letter for lack of money to buy out the landlords. Imports exceeded exports, and for the first time rice had to be purchased abroad.

In order to stimulate exports, President Macapagal removed the controls from foreign exchange and devalued the peso. In so doing he also removed one of the prime sources of graft and corruption. Then he impounded large quantities of American tobacco that had been legally admitted by his predecessor. In retaliation, the U.S. Congress threatened to reduce the Philippine sugar quota. When Congress also defeated the Philippine War Damages Claims Bill, President Macapagal cancelled a visit to the United States. At the same time he announced that henceforth the Philippine independence day would be celebrated on June 12, anniversary of the separation from Spain, rather than July 4, a date much nearer the heart of Americans. The atmosphere was heavy with anti-American tension when negotiations were undertaken on the question of criminal jurisdiction over American mili-

---

[72] Diosdado Macapagal, *Stone for the Edifice, Memoirs of a President* (Quezon City, Philippines: Mac Publishing House, 1968). Short, topical chapters give the president's own views on each of his specific problems in foreign policy.

tary personnel charged with off-duty, off-base offenses in the Philippines. Because of popular feelings aroused by the fatal shooting of Filipino trespassers at Clark Field in 1964, leftist-organized demonstrators in Manila carried the usual Yankee-go-home placards and hanged the American ambassador in effigy.

The tension was relieved appreciably by the need for better U.S.-Philippine understanding as hostilities approached in Vietnam. On July 15, 1964, Major General Nguyen Khanh, chairman of the Military Revolutionary Council of Vietnam, requested of President Macapagal all the support that was possible and opportune. After the attacks on American destroyers in the Tonkin Gulf the following month, President Macapagal reversed his previous decision and visited President Johnson in Washington. As a result of their conversations, the two presidents, noting the struggle of the people of South Vietnam against Communist aggression and its implication for all free people, reaffirmed their intention to stand by the people of Vietnam and reiterated their commitment to the defense of Southeast Asia under the SEATO treaty. President Johnson made it clear that any armed attack against the Philippines would be regarded as an attack against the American forces stationed there. He agreed to review existing programs of assistance and consider changes needed to achieve increased capability and flexibility in the Philippine response to threatened or actual aggression. For his part, President Macapagal said that the pattern for the immediate future was clear—the historic and mutually beneficial Philippine-American partnership, as it related to Philippine security, economic progress, and freedom, would continue.[73]

On his return to Manila, President Macapagal tried unsuccessfully to persuade the Philippine Congress to send troops to Vietnam. The Prime Minister of Vietnam, Dr. Phan Hay Quat, asked the Philippines for engineer troops for peaceful and constructive purposes, and President Johnson agreed to bolster the Philippines with a grant of assistance for security and intelligence purposes, but the Filipinos were as sharply divided as the Americans when it came to determining the most appropriate course of action.[74]

---

[73] U.S. Department of State, *Bulletin*, November 2, 1964, pp. 632-634.
[74] General Alfredo M. Santos, "Why We Should Send Military Aid to South Vietnam," *Philippines Free Press*, Manila, July 10, 1965. The chief of staff of the armed forces of the Philippines states the government's case.

Senate President Marcos led the opposition to the commitment of Philippine troops to Vietnam on the grounds that Macapagal was using Vietnam policy as a means of indulging his totalitarian propensities. Marcos was angry at Macapagal for welshing on his agreement not to seek reelection in 1965. Marcos had already deserted the Liberals, and he was about to run for the presidency on the Nacionalista ticket.

2

The Marcos Years

The Election of 1965

At the time of his first campaign for the presidency, Ferdinand Marcos seemed to be a typical Filipino office seeker. Intensely nationalistic and thoroughly committed to the economic and social development of his country, he also appreciated the unpalatable fact that every aspect of Philippine security and prosperity depended upon the health of the American connection.

Like other election years in the Philippines, 1965 was a continuous carnival of parades, klieg lights, fiestas, and party rallies. Newspapers, magazines, radio and television, conversations at barbershops, cocktail parties, and dinner tables featured nothing but politics. The people were asked to consider such important issues as the elimination of graft and corruption, perennial poverty, social justice, land reform, smoldering insurgency, industrialization, inflation and unemployment, the proliferation of crime and violence, the need for foreign capital, trade expansion, participation in the war in Vietnam, and the containment of international communism.

Every appeal to reason was lost in the cascade of empty oratory. Decent citizens deplored the prostitution of the democratic process: party platforms counted less than pesos and persuasion less than violence. The victory of Marcos stemmed in large part from the fact that he had a good organization with ample funds, a good slogan in "throw the rascals out," and an astute, attractive wife with tremendous crowd appeal to accompany him on the campaign trail.

The First Term of President Marcos, 1965–1969

At the beginning of his first term, President Marcos faced internal problems of crisis proportions. He described the woes of the nation in his inaugural address. The Filipino had lost his soul, his dignity, and his courage, Marcos said. Ideals had become a thin veneer for greed and power, and devotion to duty a cover for obsession with private advantage and personal gain. "We have come to the point of despair," the president said, "we have declared for peace in our time but we cannot even guarantee life and limb in our growing cities. . . . Our government is gripped in the iron hand of venality, its treasury is barren, its resources are wasted, its civil service is slothful and indifferent, its armed forces demoralized and its councils sterile."

Marcos charged that unemployment had increased, the prices of essential commodities and services had risen, and the availability of rice had become uncertain. For the future, he would demand fiscal restraint and promised that every form of waste and conspicuous consumption would be condemned as inimical to public welfare. He pledged that he would execute the law and preserve the constitution of the republic; he would work for the accomplishment of his vision, "a government that acts as the guardian of the law's majesty, the source of justice to the weak and solace to the underprivileged, a ready friend and protector of the common man, and a sensitive instrument for his advancement, not his captivity." [1]

The first term of President Marcos had scarcely begun when he launched trial balloons hinting at constitutional changes that would allow him ten or more years in the presidency. Meanwhile, Marcos turned to the United States for as much help as he could get in meeting the problems of his country and in furthering his own political ambitions. In soliciting American support, Marcos had to be careful not to alienate the extreme nationalists among the politicians, journalists, and intellectuals. Since the United States was deep in the crisis in Vietnam, he was able to formulate a Vietnam policy that would attract the assistance from the United States that he so desperately needed.

Support for U.S. Policy in Vietnam. Although as a senator Marcos had opposed Macapagal's proposal to send Philippine forces to Vietnam, as president he asked the Philippine Congress in 1966 to

---

[1] The first inaugural address by President Marcos, entitled "Mandate for Greatness," was printed and circulated by the Office of the President, Manila, 1965.

provide funds for a Philippine Civic Action Group (PHILCAG) to serve in Vietnam. This would include medical and dental teams, engineers, and appropriate security guards. Marcos had to answer such pointed questions in the Philippine Congress as "Why meddle in someone else's war" and "Why take the Vietnam monkey off the back of LBJ?" He made no public mention of secret agreements with the United States advantageous to the Philippines, or of the jobs provided for 6,000 Filipinos by the American presence in Indochina, or of the substantial profits he anticipated from increased Philippine trade with Vietnam, or of the combat training that the United States would give the Philippine army.[2]

Instead, Marcos built his case on such lofty sentiments as, "No price is too high to pay for freedom," and "The option for liberty must be held open for every country in our part of the world." It would be an insult to his people, he said, to insinuate that their convictions had been imposed upon them by any foreign power. He denied vehemently any suggestion that he was being forced or bribed by the United States in any way, but he brought Philippine foreign policy more closely in line with that of the United States than it had been since the days of Magsaysay.

Public opinion was marshaled behind the government line and the media reiterated arguments in defense of the president's position. "If the Reds win in Vietnam, that victory will signal the reactivation of communist insurgency all over Southeast Asia, including the Philippines." "Asian communists have a common policy of aggression: Korea yesterday, Vietnam today; India, Tibet and the rest of Southeast Asia tomorrow. . . . We must stop aggression here if the security of Asia and ultimately the world is to be safeguarded." "We are not going to Vietnam to kill and destroy, but on a mission of peace." "We are going to put out the fire in our neighbor's house and to rescue our friends in distress." One editorial declared, "We are sending troops in the name of collective security as a matter of honor, of national dignity and as an act of faith and because we do not want to be free loaders in the fight

---

[2] U.S. Congress, Senate, Subcommittee on United States Security Agreements and Commitments Abroad of the Committee on Foreign Relations, part 1, 1969, *Republic of the Philippines*, 91st Congress, 1st session. (Hereafter referred to as *Symington Hearings.*) Details of negotiations preceding the dispatch of PHILCAG to Vietnam are given on p. 270 ff. Intermittent press releases from Malacanang, the Philippine White House throughout the time of the hearings, took exception to parts of the evidence submitted to the Symington subcommittee.

for freedom." Another, more down to earth, said, "We must not sit on our hands—some day we may want the Americans to help us." [3]

Philippine officialdom insisted upon the importance of Vietnam to the security of the Philippines and identified itself completely with the objectives of the United States. The Marcos government took the position that if South Vietnam were allowed to fall, the chain of defense of SEATO would be broken and the day would not be far off when the Filipinos would be fighting Communists on their very shores. Shifting the focus of attention from Communists in general to Communist China as the enemy, the government held that if the United States should withdraw from Southeast Asia, there was not the slightest doubt that Communist China would seize the continent. It was argued that, by defending South Vietnam, the United States stood for the safety of all free nations in Asia and that if the Philippines should fail to participate convincingly in collective action to preserve peace and security, it would disappoint its friends and damage its image as the champion of freedom and democracy in East Asia.

The Personal Diplomacy of Marcos. The views of the Philippine government were given a hearing in Washington on the occasion of a state visit by President Marcos at the invitation of President Johnson in September 1966. This was a personal triumph for Marcos in every respect. It gave him immeasurable political prestige at home and brought him forcefully to the attention of the American public.

The address Marcos delivered to a joint session of the American Congress was in its way an oratorical masterpiece. He said at the outset that he came as an Asian, bringing a message of fraternal affection for the great American democracy that flourished in freedom and served as the trustee of civilization for all humanity. According to him, it was not yet time for the United States to lay down the heavy burden of leadership because the people of Asia still looked to the Americans for security from aggression, for economic cooperation, and for moral leadership. Since all of the non-Communist nations of Asia needed the umbrella of American power to shield them from Communist infiltration, subversion, and aggression, the hand of America must remain steady on the wheel of power and responsibility. Marcos warned Congress that after the conflict in Vietnam was settled, China would become

---

[3] The Vietnam debate was pursued in the Congress and in the media. The quotes used here are taken from successive issues of the *Philippines Free Press* which gave lengthy coverage to both sides.

48

a bigger problem, with military power to match its intransigence and expansionist ambitions, and that the might of the United States in Asia would be a necessary deterrent until a regional system of security could be developed.

Marcos went on to say that he was not afraid of any residual imperialist ambitions on the part of the United States. Whatever some of his countrymen might say, he recognized that American bases and troops were in Asia solely to deter any encroachment of Communist power in those areas; the United States was in Vietnam only to protect the independence and territorial integrity of South Vietnam, without any desire for political hegemony or economic gain.

But Marcos injected a note of bitterness into his honeyed words. Appealing for better treatment for Philippine veterans, he said, "The Filipino soldier feels disowned by you. . . . Too many of our people have long ago lost faith in your sense of fairness and . . . have given up hope of American justice." He told Congress that many Filipino critics of the United States believed that American policy was directed only at establishing the permanence and predominance of American power in Asia, at satisfying America's needs in Asia, regardless of the fate of the individual Asian.

Concluding, President Marcos asked for greater U.S. assistance to the Philippines. "The challenge to America is to extend to Asia the defensive shield of American power in forms consonant with Asians' freedom and self-respect." Describing poverty as an open gate to subversion, he declared, "Our deepest hunger is not of the body but of the spirit. Asians desire the fullest attainable measure of human equality and human dignity." His climactic appeal was, "Let America speak from the depths of its own heart: with the voice of Jefferson, the compassion of Lincoln, the vision of Roosevelt and with Kennedy's clarion call for a crusade in behalf of the weak, the oppressed and the defenseless." [4]

At the conclusion of the Marcos visit, the customary joint communiqué set forth a broad program to facilitate economic and scientific progress in the Philippines. The United States pledged expanded assistance for agricultural programs and civic action projects and promised support for measures to provide increased benefits for Philippine war veterans and their families. In addition, it was dis-

[4] The text of the address is in *Congressional Record*, September 15, 1966, vol. 112, part 17, p. 22740, Department of State, *Bulletin*, October 10, 1966, p. 535, and *U.S. News and World Report*, October 3, 1966.

covered that some $28 million remained after the accounts for the war-damage payments made in accordance with the Tydings Rehabilitation Act of 1946 were closed, and it was agreed that this money should be put to effective and creative use in a Special Education Fund to be established by the two governments.

In political matters, the United States reaffirmed its recognition of the strategic role played by the Philippines in the mutual defense network in the Western Pacific. Both governments acknowledged that the U.S. bases were necessary for mutual defense and arranged for a joint statement by Secretaries Rusk and Ramos to formalize the agreements of 1959 covering the length of the leases and conflicts of jurisdiction. The United States pledged its continued assistance in the concerted drive of the Marcos administration to improve the well-being of the people and to strengthen the armed forces for internal defense. To expand the Philippine government's capability in civic action, it was agreed that the United States would provide equipment for five engineering construction battalions and would consider equipping five more during the coming fiscal year. It was also agreed to keep the entire military assistance program under continuing review to ensure that the materiel and training supplied to the Philippine armed forces would remain appropriate to the changing requirements and missions of these forces.

On the regional and international level, the United States and the Philippines undertook to discuss ways and means for the countries in the Southeast Asian area to share their experiences in checking Communist infiltration and subversion and to consider setting up a center for the study of and possible concerted action against Communist-inspired insurgency. The United States reiterated its support for a conference of Asians to settle the Vietnam War and for the idea of a permanent Asian forum to which crises like that in Vietnam could be referred for settlement. Presidents Johnson and Marcos registered their complete agreement that the principal threat to peace and security in the Asian region was the Communist aggression in South Vietnam.[5]

After his triumphal return from Washington, President Marcos took the initiative in convening the Manila Summit Conference of the heads of the governments that had sent troops to Vietnam. The main boulevards of Manila were festooned with welcome banners for the

---

[5] Department of State, *Bulletin*, October 10, 1966, p. 531. See also U.S. Information Service, Press Release, Manila, September 16, 1966.

occasion, and Marcos clearly enjoyed the limelight that surrounded him as a leader of Asia. With American aid in his pocket, he played his role with consummate skill. He was confident that the American commitment to the Philippines augured well for his own political future and for the destiny of his country. He would be kept abreast of developments on the mainland of Asia and he was certain that the Philippines would have a voice in the shaping of post-Vietnam Southeast Asia. [6]

Yet Marcos never lost sight of the necessity for alternative Philippine policies should the Americans tire of war in Asia and retreat to Fortress America. He was aware of the teach-ins and of the bitter criticism American policy was being subjected to at home. As a precaution, he traveled to South Vietnam to reassess the situation at first hand. He visited PHILCAG in July 1967 and gave his troops the encouragement that was expected of him. At heart, however, he was very skeptical of the good they were doing.

Marcos was further disillusioned by the results of the Vietnam elections of 1967. If President Thieu could not muster more than one-third of the votes with all the regular and irregular help at his command, the future of the Thieu regime looked shaky at best. The unpleasant revelations of the Tet offensive the following year and the fading away of President Johnson from the American political scene stirred Marcos to action. He noted the growing American frustration in Vietnam and the first troop withdrawals ordered by the newly elected President Nixon. Marcos immediately pulled his own men out of Vietnam and named the veteran diplomat Carlos Romulo as his new secretary of foreign affairs.

The New Developmental Diplomacy. In 1969 President Marcos and Secretary Romulo together devised an innovative approach to Philippine foreign policy that they called the New Developmental Diplomacy.[7] Based on the Philippine people's sense of their national identity and the ideals of the United Nations, it was designed to cater to the needs of economic and social development and to reduce the excessive reliance of the Philippines upon the United States. The issue of nationalism,

---

[6] Descriptions based on the personal observations of the author, who was in Manila at the time of the summit conference.

[7] Carlos P. Romulo, "An Innovative Approach to Our Foreign Relations," issued as a pamphlet by the Department of Foreign Affairs, Manila, January 2, 1969. The views of Romulo were given extensive coverage in all the news media in Manila.

which had been in limbo since the coming to power of the Liberals under Macapagal, was revived to become the most powerful weapon in Marcos's political arsenal.

To a great extent, the Filipinos were driven to their new diplomacy by the uncertainties of American policy. During the fateful year of 1968, the Filipinos could not be sure whether the United States would escalate its efforts in Vietnam or push vigorously for peace in Paris. They had no way of knowing whether Humphrey or Nixon would win the election or what the victory of either would mean to Southeast Asia and the Philippines. Some Filipinos prophesied a mighty explosion of American power; others feared that the United States might abandon Southeast Asia entirely. Their government had to prepare for any eventuality. The root of any new Philippine policy had to be nationalism. President Marcos needed popular support to win reelection in 1969 and nationalism was a sure-fire vote-getter. The administration emphasized not antiforeignism or anticommunism but the consciousness of the Philippine people, bound by common traditions—one land, one blood, and one dream.

On assuming office on January 2, 1969, Secretary Romulo declared that the Filipinos were no longer children seeking guidance from a parent, but mature adults independently pursuing their own security and well-being. At that early date, he announced his government's determination to reexamine all aspects of relations with the United States. The treaties, pacts, and agreements into which the Philippines had entered were, he believed, no longer adequate. "They served us, but not too well," Romulo said, "they promoted our interests to a limited extent, but not enough to justify the almost unlimited advantages that accrued to others at the cost of our own self-reliance and initative." He protested that the Philippines did not want to be an outpost of any foreign power or a pawn in the politics of any country or group of countries. Relations with the United States, Japan, ANZUS, and SEATO would continue to be correct and friendly, but the Philippines, as a free, sovereign Asian nation would hold no brief for any of these except as its interests happened to coincide with those of the Philippines.

The foundation of this New Developmental Diplomacy was the need to assume a firmer posture toward the United States. Secretary Romulo addressed himself immediately to the Mutual Defense Treaty, which had stirred up so much controversy at the time of its adoption in 1951.

The administration recommended to the Philippine Congress that the treaty be revised in accordance with the old Recto formula. Instead of the clause obligating the United States to take action in accordance with its constitutional processes, the Philippines wanted the NATO-type statement that an armed attack against either of the contracting parties in the treaty area would be considered an attack against both. Hence, in the event of armed attack against the Philippines, the United States would be obligated to take immediate action to repel the attack and to restore and maintain the security of the Philippines and of the Pacific area. It was again argued that the commitment of the United States to the security of the Philippines by the Mutual Defense Treaty was so vague and so small as to be almost meaningless.

Secretary Romulo argued the need for changes in the status of the American bases, which had originally been determined by the agreement of 1947 and subjected to constant review since the administration of President Magsaysay. Romulo referred to military bases on foreign soil as states within states in violation of national sovereignty and promised that the Philippines would give the closest study to the problems of jurisdiction, taxation, customs duties, immigration rights, and relations between American military personnel and Filipinos. He took the position that it was difficult to justify the continuing presence of military bases and military defense arrangements when these were found to be inflexible in the face of changing needs. He noted the diminishing value of relying upon one's "friends" (the quotes are Romulo's) or on regional defense arrangements and said that it might be necessary to shorten the life of these arrangements or do away with them as expeditiously as the Philippines could make the adjustments necessary in connection with their termination.

The foreign secretary, who sounded more like his ancient adversary Recto than the Romulo who had espoused the cause of Philippine-American cooperation in the fifties, spoke repeatedly of the Philippines's determination to control its own economic destiny. He was firmly committed to doing away with the iniquitous parity amendment, which he lumped together with the military bases as "symbols of lingering enslavement." In his judgment, parity was neither consonant with the age-old political axiom of exclusive national rights over the inherent patrimony of a nation, nor in conformity with international sanctions of self-determination since it inhibited the state's right to determine, where Americans were concerned, who should en-

53

gage in business in the country. He expressed his approval of the approaching termination of the Laurel-Langley agreement, advocated the abandonment of all aid agreements tied up with American advice and control, and stoutly defended the Philippine policies of nationalization of retail trade and strict control of foreign investments.

While President Marcos and Secretary Romulo were revising their thinking with regard to the United States, President Nixon had begun the troop withdrawal from Vietnam and had launched his campaign for peace with honor. As the signs of the times pointed toward a lowering of the U.S. profile in Asia and the Western Pacific, the Filipinos stiffened their attitudes toward the United States.

Nevertheless, when President Nixon visited President Marcos in July 1969, the exchange of greetings gave no indication of doubt, strain, or suspicion. The presidents' words reflected only sweetness and light. President Marcos confessed his recent misgivings about the emerging policies of the United States in Asia, but he was happy to note that, while encouraging the Asian nations to pursue a nationalist course toward independence and freedom, President Nixon had showed that the United States did not intend to abandon Asia. Marcos was glad that Nixon supported the idea of Asian countries being able to defend themselves alone if necessary, but equally that Nixon was willing to extend to them whatever aid he could in times of crisis.

When President Marcos bade farewell to President Nixon at the airport, he said, "I die a small death, we die a small death, as you go and we say good-bye, but it is our hope that we shall live continuously in the friendship and affection that we have for each other."[8] Whatever the presidents might say to each other, however, many Philippine politicians gave increasing emphasis to the anti-American stand in their nationalistic pronouncements. They continued to blame an excessive individualism inherited from the Americans for weakening the traditional Filipino family system, American materialism and Protestantism for corrupting the church, American permissiveness for sapping the public morale, and American short-sightedness for causing the failure of land reform, industrialization, and the democratic system. The Manila press fanned the flames of anti-Americanism.

As the U.S. withdrawal from Vietnam continued, expressions of Philippine resentment against the United States became more emotional. Senator José Diokno charged that the bases agreement, parity, the use

---

[8] Department of State, *Bulletin,* August 25, 1969, p. 145.

of diplomatic pressure to get PHILCAG into Vietnam, and opposition to economic nationalism were all evidence of a basic American antagonism to Philippine aspirations. If the United States continued to oppose Philippine nationalism, Diokno said, there would be no further point in diplomatic dialogue.

Salvador P. Lopez, the Philippine ambassador to the United States, was among those who took advantage of the misfortunes in Vietnam to lecture the United States. He criticized the United States first for going into Vietnam and then for pulling out. He warned that the withdrawal of the United States from Southeast Asia would create a power vacuum that would cause new winds of imperialist ambition to blow from Peking and Moscow and would compel the countries in that area to make the best deal they could with the Communists. The Filipinos had been loyal allies in World War II and in the cold war, he reminded the Americans, but they would have to consider building bridges to China and Russia now that the United States was ready to quit in Asia. It was his belief that Neo-isolationism as desired by some Americans would be conceivable only if Americans would agree to throw away their rockets and nuclear weapons and return to the era of the spinning wheel and the flint-lock gun. Ambassador Lopez's final admonition was that if the United States should withdraw into Fortress America, the Indians, Japanese, Thais, Burmese, Laotians, Vietnamese, and Filipinos—all the non-Communists in Asia—would have to decide whether it was indeed better to be red than dead.[9]

The New Diplomacy in Action. The government of the Philippines lost no time in translating the philosophy of the new diplomacy into action, primarily through its efforts to stress the Asian identity of the Philippines and to take a more active part in regional cooperation. Despite his latent fear of the rebirth of Japanese militarism, as soon as the announcement of the new policy was made, Marcos launched an intensive campaign to attract Japanese assistance for the economic development of the Philippines. He wanted Japanese capital investments primarily to offset his dependence upon the Americans. He also moved

---

[9] Ambassador Lopez made many speeches in the United States expressing these and similar sentiments. Their texts are available from the Philippine Embassy, Washington. Ambassador Lopez, after leaving the Washington embassy, became president of the University of the Philippines. In 1975 he apparently displeased President Marcos and gave up the presidency of the university to return to teaching. See correspondent Bernard Wideman's interview with Ambassador Lopez, *Far Eastern Economic Review*, June 6, 1975, p. 32.

cautiously to loosen the ties between the Philippines and Taiwan and to undertake his own détente with the People's Republic of China. This was a dramatic reversal of the China policy that the Philippines had followed consistently since independence, and it offended most of the ethnic Chinese resident in the Philippines who were capitalist to the core. Indignant at the new policy, they asked the Philippine president how he could possibly approach Peking in a friendly spirit while he fought Maoist insurgents at home.

It was also during his first term in office that President Marcos began his open-door policy toward all Socialist countries. The Philippines, he announced in 1969, would pursue an independent course of friendliness and of openness even toward the Soviet Union. He would not reject ties with any country that sought ties with the Philippines, wished the Philippines no harm, and was willing to abide by the freedom of the Philippines and respect its integrity. In the interest of a new economic policy attuned to a world no longer constrained by the cold war, he pledged a new effort to expand markets and sources of imports, attract capital investments and loans, and promote cultural and economic exchanges with the Socialist world.

Marcos kept pace with President Nixon in the politics of détente. He encouraged unofficial visits by Philippine journalists and congressmen to the Chinese mainland and welcomed their reports, free as they were believed to be from the prejudices of the Americans.[10] No official visitors from mainland China visited the Philippines, but Marcos treated the Bolshoi dancers from the Soviet Union as distinguished guests. Clearly, his objective was to give himself another option in the event that Washington should terminate or relax its opposition to the Communists.

Turning to Southeast Asia, the Philippine government supported the expansion of SEATO's nonmilitary activities. The Philippines contributed to the establishment of the Asia Development Bank and became a charter member of the Asia-Pacific Council. After the fall of Sukarno and the appearance of the well-entrenched Suharto regime in Indonesia, the Philippines worked successfully with Thailand, Malaysia, Singapore, and Indonesia to convert the moribund Association of Southeast Asia into a rejuvenated Association of Southeast Asian Nations (ASEAN) for the promotion of regional cooperation.

---

[10] Teodoro M. Locsin and Nick Joaquin, "Reports on Red China," *Philippines Free Press*, beginning April 2, 1966 and July 1, 1967.

The Philippines looked upon regionalism not only as an instrument of anticommunism but also as a hedge against overdependence on the United States. If the Philippines could avoid wasteful rivalry for foreign capital with other developing countries, it could increase its bargaining power with the United States, and if it could pool its resources and technical skills with those of its neighbors, it would have less need of the United States in the war against poverty and disease. Above all, if the Philippines could create a viable regional security system, it would have no need for U.S. military bases, military assistance, or any other special arrangement with the United States. Most important in the immediate future, the combined military strength of the nations of the region would constitute a respectable force that would have to be considered in any proposed equilibrium of powers after Vietnam. Such considerations as these were calculated to allow the Philippines some measure of influence if not of control in a rapidly changing political situation.

The Second Term of President Marcos, 1969–1973

In spite of his political skill and his new diplomatic initiatives, President Marcos was not able to arrest the descent of the Philippines toward internal chaos. He won reelection in 1969, but the exercise revealed the extent of the rot in the democratic structure. It was commonly alleged that the cost of victory through the distribution of pork-barrel funds led the government to the brink of bankruptcy. The electoral campaign was marred by violence and terrorism, in spite of Marcos's use of the armed forces to keep order. The candidates dispensed promises devoid of substance, and both parties were accused of stuffing the ballot boxes, falsifying the returns, and using every other trick in the democratic book in the race for office.[11]

President Marcos's second inaugural address at the end of 1969 seemed curiously ambiguous in the light of coming events. He called for discipline and dedication in building the nation. The leadership, he pledged, would exemplify integrity and simplicity and in the next few years would lay the foundation for a revolutionary reform of international and domestic policies. Rich wasters would be chastised, extravagance avoided, and complacency scorned. "I will not demand more of you," Marcos declared, "than I demand of myself and the government— neither wealth nor power shall purchase privilege." What was more,

[11] *The Fookien Times Yearbook* (Manila: The Fookien Times, 1970), p. 76, gives a good but restrained description of the election of 1969. Contemporary issues of the *Philippines Free Press* are far more critical of the processes of that election.

the president promised to eliminate subversion without endangering liberties so as to prove to posterity that the wave of the future was not totalitarianism but democracy.[12]

Impending Crisis. During President Marcos's second term, the economic and social crisis kept pace with the political decline. The president selectively attacked the oligarchs as the primary cause of the trouble: he drew a bead on such powerful families as the Lopez, Laurel, Osmena, and Araneta clans, who were well known as his political rivals, but exempted from his denunciation the sugar barons with whom he was friendly. Similarly, he divided rich and influential Chinese and Americans into the good and the bad depending on whether they supported or opposed his personal plans.

As the population of the Philippines passed the 40 million mark, the per capita income scarcely reached $250 per year. While the rich got richer, some 300,000 squatter families in Manila alone existed in poverty. The land reform program adopted during the Macapagal administration had failed to relieve the misery of the agricultural areas, and the rising middle class of sharp young lawyers and businessmen showed far more eagerness to take its place among the rich than to help the poor. Industrialization lagged and domestic trade failed to bring about prosperity except for a small proportion of the people. The GNP scarcely managed to keep ahead of the rate of population growth. The balance of payments was negative and foreign capital shied away from the Philippines. Financial reserves dwindled and government expenditures far exceeded income. The bleak economic situation, dramatized by the glaring disparity between rich and poor, exacerbated endemic social unrest.[13]

One of the sources of the social instability that prevailed was precisely the attempt that many enlightened Filipinos were making to discover their own cultural identity, vitalize their political independence, and move toward more general economic welfare. They clamored for modernization—but their values, ideas, and techniques were so varied as to preclude any concerted effort to achieve common goals. The demand for change came from across the political spectrum all the way

---

[12] C. V. Fonacier, *At the Helm of the Nation* (Manila: National Media Production Center, Republic of the Philippines, 1973), p. 124 ff.

[13] Benigno S. Aquino, Jr., "What's Wrong with the Philippines," *Foreign Affairs* (New York: Council on Foreign Relations, 1968), vol. 46, October 1968, pp. 770-779.

from the loyal opposition to the extremist Maoist New People's Army, which called for the overthrow of the government and the entire capitalist establishment. All sectors of society—peasants, workers, students, professional groups, and the church—were aroused and restless. Their impatience with the lack of social justice was bound to produce an excess of criminality and the breakdown of law and order. The fundamental question was whether the conflict of social forces in a state of violent flux could be solved under controlled conditions or whether it would culminate in revolution.[14]

Landless tenants continued to harass the landlords and the government authorities. Urban laborers complained more bitterly than ever but lacked the power to strike, and the colorful rhetoric of the press was empty and ineffective. Only the students took up the cry against feudalism, fascism, and imperialism, organizing themselves into a dozen radical societies, each fiercely jealous of the others. Two schools, the Lyceum and the University of the Philippines, were singled out by the authorities as seedbeds of communism. On an ill-fated day in January 1970, students gathered in front of Malacanang, the Philippine White House, to stage a mock burial ceremony for the president and first lady and hurled rocks and bottles at the official residence. Turned away by firehoses, the mob surged to the gates of the American embassy, chanting the perennial, "Yankee Go Home." For all their rallies and demonstrations, however, the students gave no evidence of the selflessness and dedication that seem to be prerequisites for successful revolutionary movements. Their calls for reform lacked conviction, and no leaders emerged, even among the Communists, to provide the inspiration and drive that a successful antigovernment campaign would have required.[15]

To cope with the situation, President Marcos called a special election for a new constitutional convention in 1970. No one could see how a mere change in institutional framework could rectify a calamitous situation rooted in spiritual bankruptcy and corruption. No constitution could guarantee good government if it were deliberately violated. Nevertheless, President Marcos directed the political energies of his

---

[14] George M. Guthrie, ed., *Six Perspectives on the Philippines* (Manila: Bookmark, 1971). Excellent analysis of complex internal conditions by six well-qualified experts.

[15] *The Fookien Times Yearbook*, 1970, p. 76. All the daily papers and the *Philippines Free Press* for the week after January 26, 1970 carried graphic, almost lurid, accounts of the demonstrations.

people, in a time of crisis, toward the legal bickering that would inevitably characterize the long, drawn out process of drafting a new fundamental law of the land. The suspicion grew that the president was having a new constitution drafted in order to prolong his own term in office, either through the adoption of an amendment permitting him a third term or through a shift to a parliamentary system under which Mrs. Marcos, for example, might be elected president and her husband remain as prime minister for as long as he could muster a political majority.

The regular congressional elections of 1971, featuring a test of strength between President Marcos and Senator Benigno Aquino, the charismatic, rising young Liberal leader, were marred by a bombing incident during a Liberal party rally in Manila. As a consequence the president suspended the writ of habeas corpus on August 21, 1971 in view of the danger of subversion or insurrection and hinted at the possibility of martial law.[16] The president's party was defeated decisively at the polls in November, but Marcos was not one to sit idly by while his troubles multiplied. He looked to the United States for sympathy and a certain amount of assistance but stopped short of inviting American intervention in his internal struggles. He had no wish for the Philippines to become another Vietnam. While secretly charting his own future course, he prepared to take decisive action to halt his country's progressive deterioration.[17]

Marcos could hardly blame his political enemies for the woes of his people. He himself had been too long at the helm of the ship of state. It was he who had appointed the men who occupied positions of power in the armed forces and the constabulary or who, once elected to high posts with his help, had failed to meet their responsibilities. His own kinsmen and compadres held positions of influence in the bureaucracy, which was honeycombed with graft and corruption. He was at least as much at fault as anyone else for the plight of the Philippines on the eve of martial law.

---

16 *Philippines Free Press*, September 4, 1971, began a series of articles entitled "Democracy—Philippine Style," which foreshadowed the coming clash between President Marcos and Senator Aquino. The article of September 11 was entitled "No Quarter for Ninoy?" "Ninoy" is Aquino's nickname.

17 *Philippines Free Press*, November 20, 1971. Three lead articles were devoted to the victory of the Liberal party. At this time President Marcos published his book *Today's Revolution: Democracy* (Manila: Office of the President, 1971), blaming the radicals and the Communists for chaos and terror and previewing his program, which he described as democracy's challenge to revolution.

By September 23, 1972—the effective date of the proclamation of martial law—the country was teetering on the brink of disaster. Luis Taruc, the former leader of the Huks, who was free after having served his twelve-year sentence in jail, said, "There are signs a revolution is beginning. I have traveled the country over and I have seen the signs. It has not yet reached the critical stage, but the signs are there."[18] The president himself pointed out that national and local governments had become paralyzed, the productive sectors of the economy had ground to a halt, and the judiciary had become unable to dispense justice. The level of crime had escalated beyond the capability of the local police and civilian authorities to deal with it, and citizens were afraid to leave their houses.

The city of Manila was in the grip of fear and lawlessness. Kidnapping increased, students were killed in the midst of demonstrations, bomb scares multiplied, and the plush Philippine-American Life Insurance Company and the Hilton Hotel were among the buildings actually bombed.

The government failed utterly in its campaign for law and order in rice-rich Luzon. Thirty-three out of thirty-seven municipalities in the province of Isabela alone were reported to be in the control of the Communist party and the New People's Army. As the armed forces, the constabulary, and the Barrio Self-Defense Units—the village militia—all failed to overcome the armed insurgents, local political leaders raised their own feudal-style private armies for self-protection. The villagers were caught in a reign of terror. In the southern Philippines, meanwhile, parts of Mindanao, Palawan, Basilan, and the Sulu Archipelago were plunged into violent disorder by battles between government forces and Muslim dissidents. The rebellious Muslims together with local bandits and a small number of adherents of the New People's Army created a state of disorder bordering on civil war in the southern Philippines.[19]

It was difficult to say whether the patient was half alive or half dead. For all its suffering, the Philippine body politic gave evidence of residual strength and inner vitality. A study of the Philippines by the Rand Corporation on the eve of martial law concluded that the political

---

[18] Conversation with author at home of a mutual friend in Manila. Taruc later voiced these same thoughts during his lectures in the United States.

[19] This picture is not overdrawn. See, for example, Robert Shaplen, "Letter from Manila," in the *New Yorker*, April 14, 1973, and David F. Roth, "Deterioration and Reconstruction of National Political Parameters: The Philippines during the 1970's," *Asian Survey*, September 1973.

system appeared to be stable and generally responsive to the desires of most people, the economy appeared to be performing better than commonly thought, crime was not a national problem because violence and fear of violence were concentrated in a few areas, and dissident groups were not a serious threat to the government. The Rand report served as an antidote to the spate of journalistic accounts that tended to over-emphasize the nation's troubles. Reforms were needed, it was generally agreed, but they scarcely called for the destruction of the democratic system.[20]

U.S. Assistance to the Marcos Regime. President Marcos was aware that his New Developmental Diplomacy might result in an aggravation of local insurgency and give offense to the United States. He discussed his problems with President Nixon on the occasion of Nixon's visit to Manila in July 1969. Marcos acknowledged that the roots of insurgency lay in economic and social injustice and that what he needed to cope with internal subversion was a viable economy, sound political policies, and strong armed forces. Nevertheless, external factors were also involved. The objectives of his diplomatic measures, therefore, were to minimize the outside support made available to the insurgents and to obtain as much help as he could from the United States. The less he was obliged to spend on putting down insurgents, the more he would have for internal reform. Marcos asked Nixon for nothing more than the fulfillment of commitments pledged under solemn treaties.[21] He made no mention of which commitments or which treaties he had in mind, and no further public reference was made to any specific request for American help.

During his second term in office, Marcos continued to rely heavily upon assistance from the United States. His program of giving the people rice, roads, and schools would have been ineffective without American grants of assistance, advice, equipment, and machinery. The United States also provided substantial military supplies and equipment

---

[20] Harvey A. Averch, John E. Koehler, and Frank H. Denton, *The Matrix of Policy in the Philippines* (Princeton: Princeton University Press, 1971). This study, sponsored by the U.S. Agency for International Development, stresses the point that the problems of crime, insurgency, political instability, and poor economic performance were "exaggerated, or imaginary or different in important ways from the manner in which they had been generally understood" (from the introduction, p. 1).

[21] Department of State, *Bulletin*, August 25, 1969, p. 145.

and gave the Philippine forces extensive training in civic action.[22] Americans working for the military and the Central Intelligence Agency were restricted from combat zones in Luzon and Mindanao, but they simulated combat situations in comparable localities for training purposes. The national police administration received U.S. computer equipment for the identification and apprehension of criminal elements or political dissidents, and many Philippine policemen were given advanced, specialized training in the United States.[23]

Many Filipinos criticized Marcos for his excessive reliance upon the United States as well as for his treatment of domestic matters. The critics accused him of making no real effort to attack the fundamental ills of the Philippines and contenting himself with a show of force against elements that had genuine reason to oppose the government. Continued American assistance, they argued, impeded national progress by allowing the government to rely upon military means to cope with a

---

[22] U.S. Congress, House, Committee on International Relations, Subcommittee on International Organizations, *"Human Rights in South Korea and the Philippines: Implications for U.S. Policy,"* 94th Congress, 1st session, 1975. (Hereafter referred to as House of Representatives, *Hearings on Human Rights.)* See page 317 for details on Military Assistance to the Government of the Philippines, 1970-1975.

	In millions of dollars (for fiscal years)					
	1970	1971	1972	1973	1974	1975
Military Assistance Program	15.0	16.0	12.9	15.9	15.4	20.4
Training	.9	.9	1.1	.8	.5	.6
Credits (Foreign Military Sales)	—	—	—	—	8.6	7
Excess Defense Articles	.6	5.2	1.4	4.3	15	2.5
JUSMAG	1.6	1.4	1.3	1.5	1.6	1.6
Total	18.21	23.5	16.7	22.5	41.1	32.1

[23] For an interesting article on U.S. participation in law enforcement activities in the Philippines, see Geoffrey Arlin, "The Organizers," in *Far Eastern Economic Review*, July 2, 1973, p. 16. This article describes U.S. aid in reorganizing, funding, and training the Philippine police apparatus and concludes that without U.S. aid, President Marcos could not have made martial law a success. George Kahin, in his testimony to the Senate Foreign Relations Committee, "U.S. Commitment to SEATO" March 6, 1974, p. 31, quotes the National Survey of Major Religious Superiors to the effect that in the Visayas the presence of U.S. military personnel directing the antidissident campaign on Panay has been confirmed by very reliable sources. It was stated that "American army men in uniform are working on the road from Ilo Ilo to Capiz. This is N.P.A. (New People's Army)-infected territory so people wonder why." See also Benedict John Kerkvliet, Fellow, Woodrow Wilson International Center for Scholars, Smithsonian Institution, in U.S. Congress, House of Representatives, *Hearings before the Subcommittee on Asian and Pacific Affairs of the Committee on Foreign Affairs*, 93rd Congress, 2nd session, May 1 and June 5, 1974, "Political Prisoners in South Vietnam and the Philippines" (p. 73 ff.). Kerkvliet repeatedly alleges that American support made martial law possible. The State Department questioned Professor Kerkvliet's testimony (p. 87 ff) and the scholarly standards upon which it was based.

nonmilitary social ailment. They began to fear that the president might resort to dictatorship to control a situation that he could not cure, and they hastened to censure the United States for putting the necessary weapons in his hands. American support, they charged, gave Marcos the muscle to stay in power.[24]

Public opinion toward the United States during the second term of President Marcos was tinged with hostility. The administration itself was ambivalent, relying heavily upon the United States for assistance while vociferously condemning American policies. It was still the official line that the wretched quality of life in the Philippines was the result of colonial bondage, and some of the more nationalistic politicians and journalists called repeatedly for the complete abolition of American bases and withdrawal of American forces, an end to economic privileges for Americans, and the nationalization of all American enterprises.

The immediate cause for criticism of the United States in the latter days of the second administration of President Marcos was the course of the war in Vietnam, which was painful to the United States and embarrassing to the Philippines as an American ally. Many Filipinos were chagrined by the revelations of the Symington hearings, which had made it appear that PHILCAG was nothing more than an American mercenary force.[25] The Filipinos were deriving as little glory as the Americans from the Indochina hostilities, and they condemned the American bombing, resented the association of the American bases in the Philippines with the Vietnam War, and disapproved of the widening war in Cambodia and Laos. Like many Americans, many Filipinos would have liked to be able to forget the whole Vietnam experience.

Yet many liberal Filipinos, more angry at their own feudal oligarchs than at the American "imperialists," were deeply ambivalent about the United States. On the one hand, they argued that the United States should get out of the Philippines lock, stock, and barrel; on the other hand they wanted the Americans to stay. They disliked what they believed was an unholy alliance between the Marcos administration

---

[24] Senator Aquino became the most prominent of the critics of President Marcos. It was commonly believed that Senator Aquino would become the nominee of the Liberal party for president in 1973 and that he would beat Marcos or any other Nacionalista in a regular presidential election.

[25] See U.S. Congress, Senate, Staff Report for the Committee on Foreign Relations, *Korea and the Philippines: November 1972*, 93rd Congress, 1st session, February 18, 1973. This report is a well-balanced analysis of conditions in the Philippines at the time of the proclamation of martial law.

and its American backers; they wished that Americans with their wealth and power would force the government to change its ways for the benefit of economic development and social welfare. The Americans, such liberals believed, would be their last hope against a possible indigenous fascist movement; to prevent such a movement's seizing power, they would want more not less intervention in Philippine affairs. Their ideas were still nebulous when, on September 23, 1972, President Marcos placed the country under martial law.

Martial Law

The reason for the imposition of martial law, Marcos announced, was the

> threat from lawless elements who are moved by a common or similar ideological conviction, design, strategy and goal and enjoying the active moral and material support of a foreign power . . . who are staging, undertaking and waging an armed insurrection and rebellion . . . to supplant our existing political, social, economic and legal order with an entirely new one whose form of government . . . and whose political, social, economic, legal and moral precepts are based on the Marxist-Leninist-Maoist teachings and beliefs.[26]

What Marcos was referring to in these general terms was the threat posed by the endemic rural insurgents, now labeled a Communist conspiracy linked with the New People's Army, the Muslim independence movement, a Christian Socialist agrarian reform movement, and a recently uncovered rightist plan for a coup d'état and revolution. The rightist plot had allegedly been concocted by a cabal of ex-colonels and ex-generals who intended to discredit the president, assassinate him, and overthrow the government. The key figures in the plot were alleged to be Vice President Lopez and former presidential candidate Sergio Osmena, Jr. These men had recruited supporters, it was claimed by government spokesmen, from the armed forces and civilian agencies and had established a liaison with the New People's Army and various leftist student and labor groups. The actual assassin or "hit man" was

---

[26] Office of the President of the Philippines, *Proclamation 1081*, September 22, 1972.

to be an American. The American embassy had allegedly been informed of the plot before its discovery by the Marcos government, but this the embassy heatedly denied.[27]

President Marcos judged the situation to be sufficiently grave to warrant his assuming total power and total responsibility for the indefinite future. He insisted that it was more important to save the Philippines than to preserve the form of government that had been in operation for three-quarters of a century. His previous declarations in praise of freedom and democracy notwithstanding, he proclaimed a benign authoritarian regime that would restore law and order and create a "new society."

Revolution from the Right. President Marcos ruled the country through a succession of decrees, orders, and letters of instruction. He conceived of his program as a "revolution from the right" that would bring to an end the outmoded Anglo-Saxon concepts of freedom and American-style democracy. He made no pretense that he was merely suspending the old order, which had guaranteed civil rights, but let it be known that he would evolve an entirely new philosophy of rights and obligations that would be responsive to the Philippine rather than the American experience. He suspended the Congress and closed down the free press, radio, and television, ordered the disbandment of private armies and the surrender of unlicensed firearms, discharged one-tenth of the 60,000 civil servants for graft and incompetence, and jailed thousands of dangerous characters of the right and left without formal charges. Political rivals, including Senators Aquino and Diokno, and some fifteen leading newspaper publishers and columnists were among those

---

[27] In a letter to Ambassador Romualdez in Washington dated June 26, 1975, the secretary of national defense declared: "the government has in its possession more than sufficient evidence to support criminal charges against Messers. Lopez, Jr. and Osmena III." House of Representatives, *Hearings on Human Rights*, p. 429. For defense of Lopez, see statement of Gerald N. Hill, attorney at law for the Lopez family, in the same *Hearings*, p. 289 ff. An AP report from Manila, May 24, 1975, published on that date in many American newspapers including the *New York Times*, stated that August McCormick Lehman, Jr., an American who had been under detention for thirty-two months, told military investigators that he had been introduced as a "top killer for the Mafia" to former Senator Serge Osmena, Jr., one of the "brains of the plot" to assassinate Marcos in 1972. A U.P.I. report from Manila, as published in the *San José Mercury*, February 10, 1977, stated Lehman was sentenced to six years imprisonment at hard labor and fined $1,420 by the military tribunal.

detained.[28] The universities were raided and public utilities taken over by the armed forces. These measures were carried out with a minimum of brutality.

The president took immediate steps to place his regime on a firm constitutional and legal basis. Having finally obtained a draft from the constitutional convention, he offered it on January 15, 1973 to 30,000 handpicked citizen assemblies throughout the islands for their approval. This procedure he called *barangay* or grass-roots democracy. On the strength of a 90 percent affirmative vote by show of hands, Marcos declared the new constitution adopted but temporarily suspended. He based his right to govern on provisions of the new constitution that call for the incumbent president to exercise full authority pending the convening of an interim National Assembly at the president's direction. Periodically Marcos asked the citizens to show their hands in open meeting if they wanted him to stay in office to finish the job he had begun. Inevitably, he received nearly unanimous support. On September 17, 1974, the Supreme Court formally approved the constitutionality of martial law, which eliminated any potential political opposition to Marcos's authoritarian tactics.[29] On October 17, 1976, President Marcos conducted his fourth referendum seeking popular approval and received a 90 percent endorsement. As locally observed, there was no way to measure the degree of apathy, cynicism, or resentment on the part of the voters.[30]

President Marcos took complete command of the government and the administration. To broaden his power base, he appointed more of his cronies and compadres to strategic positions in the army, constabu-

---

[28] Ambassador Mutuc, in the U.S. House of Representatives, *Hearings on Human Rights*, p. 286, stated that a few weeks after the proclamation of martial law about 30,000 people were arrested and detained. Senators Rodrigo and Adevoso and prominent journalists including Teodoro Locsin, Joaquin Roces, Maximo Soliven, and Napoleon Rama were among those temporarily detained. Mutuc said that by June 1974 the number of those in custody had been reduced to a mere 10,000 and by May 1975 to 6,000.

[29] In the case of *Javellana* vs. *the Executive Secretary*, the Supreme Court held on March 31, 1973, that there was "no further judicial obstacle to the new constitution being considered in force and effect." In *Benigno S. Aquino* vs. *Secretary Juan Ponce Enrile, et al.*, the Supreme Court on September 17, 1974, affirmed the validity of Proclamation 1081 when it held that a "state of rebellion existed in the country when said Proclamation was issued" and further that "the state of rebellion continues up to the present." Memorandum of the Secretary of National Defense of the Philippines, June 6, 1975, quoted in U.S. House of Representatives, *Hearings on Human Rights*, p. 362.

[30] Harvey Stockwin, "The Yes, but . . . Referendum," *Far Eastern Economic Review*, October 22, 1976.

lary, cabinet offices, and special agencies until his personal appointees staffed every provincial, municipal, and local government establishment. He increased the size and importance of the armed forces, enrolled additional thousands in the constabulary and village militias, and integrated the home defense and local police units into a National Police Commission headed by the secretary of national defense. Such "reforms" were thorough enough to forestall any danger of effective military opposition.

Within a matter of weeks, the new regime was able to claim a record of solid achievements. Law and order had returned. The incidence of crimes of violence had decreased substantially and the surface of Philippine life was pleasantly brightened. Some of the detainees were released from custody—and the national economy took a decided swing for the better. A new land reform program got under way and business was helped by tax reforms and new investment incentives. The trade balance shifted in favor of the Philippines and the tourist business boomed as life in Manila became more attractive. Whatever resistance there was to martial law had to be nursed in silence. In many quarters optimism prevailed, giving rise to the dream that the Philippines might well be the site of the next economic miracle in Asia.[31]

A Balance Sheet. Its auspicious beginning was by no means a guarantee that the new regime would be accepted for an indefinite period of time. President Marcos would stand or fall on his record of coping with economic and political problems. Total responsibility came with absolute power. If he should fail to live up to popular expectations, a public long accustomed to democratic rights would be quick to register effective protest. The fate of martial law would depend on the balance sheet of the regime's actual performance.

The first tests came in the economic sphere. It would take time to show any progress in dealing with the fundamental problems of overpopulation and mass poverty, but the new regime plunged immediately into an ambitious program of land reform. Its objective was to transfer 3.75 million acres of rice and corn land in Luzon from well-to-do landlords to the 915,000 impoverished tenants and sharecroppers who worked the land. This program covered about one-third of the

---

31 Philip Bowring, "Asia's Next Miracle?" *Far Eastern Economic Review*, September 3, 1973, p. 38. See also the paid advertisement of the government of the Philippines in *Fortune*, July 1976.

country's agricultural land but made no attempt to improve conditions on sugar or coconut plantations. The idea was to give the tenants either title to the land they tilled or to provide satisfactory leasing arrangements. Nothing was done for the 3 million or so landless agricultural workers who were at the very bottom of the poverty ladder. Substantial progress was made on about half the program in the first four years of martial law. In addition to some 200,000 lease arrangements which were satisfactorily concluded, an equal number of land-transfer certificates were issued. A certificate was given the tenant when the terms of transfer were agreed upon or when the down payment was made. The landlord received total compensation from the Land Bank, partly in cash and partly in government bonds, but he still would have preferred to keep his land. The land-transfer certificate was not the title to the land, which was to remain with the Land Bank until all the annual payments—in most cases fifteen—were made.

The land reform program represented a gigantic effort but it could not solve all the difficulties of the rural Philippines. The landlords as a group were alienated from the government and the smallest landlords affected—those owning from seventeen to sixty acres—were able to prevent the application of the program to their holdings. They found many ways to get around the land reform decrees.[32] The peasants discovered that it was a lot easier to make the first payment than to meet subsequent ones and that it was often more difficult than they had imagined to discharge the responsibilities of ownership—upkeep of the property, management of their capital, costs of fertilizers and pesticides, and cooperative marketing. They missed the advantages they had enjoyed under the landlord-tenant relationship. The government, for its part, discovered that the costs of financing the program were astronomical, even aside from the burdens of irrigation, reclamation projects, and the construction of badly needed rural highways. Land reform did not automatically increase the level of production nor did it necessarily contribute to the popularity of martial law in the countryside. Even so confirmed a radical as Luis Taruc, however, gave President Marcos good marks for striking at the roots of the economic and social injustice that had long plagued the Philippines.[33]

---

[32] Robert Shaplen, "Letter from Manila," *New Yorker*, May 3, 1976. See also Far Eastern Economic Review, *Asia Yearbook, 1977*, section on the Philippines, p. 273 ff.

[33] Tom Weber, "The Lingering Power of a Former Rebel," *San Francisco Chronicle*, October 22, 1976.

Public confidence in the government spurred every phase of business activity, and as a result of higher revenue collections the administration increased its expenditures for national development, especially in rural areas. More foreign capital was attracted to the Philippines by a favorable investments incentive policy. The GNP registered a constant growth rate of nearly 6 percent. The government worked hard to make the country self-sufficient in food and it spent immense sums in new construction in and around Manila. Fourteen new hotels, a luxurious culture center, convention center, folk art theater, and condominiums for the affluent built largely from government funds gave downtown Manila the misleading appearance of unprecedented prosperity.

But the balance of trade, rosy in 1973 and less so in 1974, turned downward in 1975 and remained negative in 1976. The deficit in the international balance of payments was estimated at $200 million in 1976 and was forecast to be the same in 1977 if the price of imported oil rose by no more than 10 percent and if sugar brought in eleven cents per pound on the export market. Much of the deficit in merchandise trade, over $1 billion in 1975 and $878 million in 1976, was made up by the profits from invisible items such as the tourist trade and service transactions and by capital transfers. The current-account deficit in 1976 amounted to the substantial figure of $534 million, slightly below the record current-account deficit of $573 million recorded in 1975. At the end of 1976, the nation's external debt stood at $5,554 million, up by $1,804 million in a single year, but its accumulated financial reserves still amounted to $1,143 million, an increase of some $50 million in 1976.[34] The government seemed to be in basically sound financial condition since it was able to borrow at a reasonable rate of interest and it reported that a foreign-credit line of $1 billion was available at any time to support the peso. Nevertheless, the Center of Research and Communications in Manila projected that even with stable prices in international commerce the twin spectres of inflation and devaluation would haunt the economy for the next five years.[35]

After four years of martial law, President Marcos encountered his greatest economic challenge in the management of the sugar industry. Practically every stage of sugar production in the Philippines is controlled and financed by the government. In 1974, with sugar at sixty-

[34] Leo Gonzaga, "A Tougher Year for Manila," *Far Eastern Economic Review*, January 14, 1977.
[35] Leo Gonzaga, "Philippine Anxieties," *Far Eastern Economic Review*, November 26, 1976.

five cents per pound on the world market, the government reaped in the profits and the planters, with the help of Japanese capital, expanded their acreage and built new mills at a dizzy pace. Hoping for still greater increases in the price of sugar, the government held off in sales and piled up a huge surplus of sugar in the warehouses. When the price unexpectedly tumbled to a low of nine cents per pound, the government was obliged to unload, selling some 600,000 metric tons to the Soviet Union and 450,000 tons to the People's Republic of China. With no money available for current operations, the planters could not even pay their workers the paltry guaranteed wages of seven pesos (one dollar) per day. With a total of 431,000 sugar workers living in conditions amounting to voluntary bondage, the situation in the sugar lands of the Visayas, Central Philippines, assumed ominous proportions. Hard pressed to survive within the law, the workers were increasingly tempted to cast their lot with the New People's Army.[36]

Industry, too, faced growing difficulties. Because the rate of corporate expansion and foreign investment slowed down significantly after 1974, the short- and medium-term prospects looked dim for manufacturing, processing, and assembly industries which were oriented toward the domestic market and heavily dependent on imports for raw material and machinery. Industrial growth brought greater profits for the favored few but meant little for the workers, whose real wages declined from base 100 in 1965 to an index of 70 in 1975. In spite of vigorous anti-inflation policies, prices increased by about 7 percent in 1975 and 1976. As the government budget expanded, the tax rate went up and government became ever more deeply embroiled in the private sector. Official figures showed that unemployment fell from 7.9 percent before martial law to 3.8 percent in 1976, but the criteria for measuring employment were overly generous. Effective unemployment (inability to work enough to earn a minimum wage) reached 15 percent by 1976. Even a short sojourn in the fishing villages along the rivers or the coast, a visit to the humble homes of the rural poor, or a stroll through the slums of Manila discloses how much remains to be done by any regime, democratic or otherwise, in order to relieve poverty.[37]

---

[36] George McArthur, "A Philippine Boom that Got out of Hand," *San Francisco Chronicle*, December 2, 1976; "Easing Philippine Sugar Problems," *Far Eastern Economic Review*, February 4, 1977, p. 40.

[37] *Asia Year Book, 1977*, p. 276 for useful summary of the current state of the Philippine economy. See also Derek Davies, "State of the Union," and Rodney Tasker, "State of the Economy," *Far Eastern Economic Review*, February 11, 1977, pp. 16-20.

The political test of martial law was: how much repression would the Filipino people stand and for how long while President Marcos wrestled with his internal problems? When martial law was imposed, 5,000 arrests were made, and of those 4,000 were arrests by legal warrants of ordinary criminals with no connection to any political movement. The remaining 1,000 were arrested and detained, with or without formal charges, and were held only because of their opposition to Marcos or his government. A two-man mission of Amnesty International reported in July 1976 that torture was part of a general approach to the treatment of suspects, but Marcos insisted that torture was not a policy, although some incidents had occurred, as the military itself admitted.[38] The president claimed that any soldier or official who extracted confessions or statements by force was punished and that on that basis he had dismissed 19 officers and 300 soldiers by November 1976. By that time, he said, 1,000 of those in custody had been released and about 200 or 300 of those still held were charged with subversion, treason, or outright murder. Nobody was being arrested, according to the president, unless there was a case against him based on legal evidence, and everyone under detention was facing a case in court.[39]

Filipinos who personally prospered under martial law tended to join the chorus of approval; many former government critics scuttled their beliefs for the sake of well-paying jobs in the administration. Journalists, politicians, intellectuals, or oligarchs who found it impossible to fall in line with *barangay* democracy, meanwhile, were doomed to exist in a state of fear, not knowing when they might incur the wrath of the authorities. Most important, a large number of intelligent people were not won over to the new regime that had torn the government from them and placed it in the hands of a single man. People and government had assumed a "we" and "they" relationship. While the people appreciated the good things that were given them, they did not fail to notice what they had lost.

The national goose step became more prevalent as more and more spheres of activity fell under the fiat of Malacanang, the Philippine White House. Absolute conformity was the price of law and order, silence the only course for those who hated the system and had to work

---

38 The report of Amnesty International is available from Amnesty International publications, 53 Theobald's Road, London WC IX, 8 S P England.
39 *U.S. News and World Report*, November 22, 1976, p. 65.

within it. Filipinos with long memories were reminded of life under the Japanese occupation, only this time the apparatus of totalitarianism was in the hands of Filipinos themselves.

The Philippine nation was deprived of the talents of thousands of its own well-educated, high-spirited citizens. How was such a loss to be measured against the gains of improved law and order and selective prosperity? In addition to the strictly political prisoners, thousands of people were placed under house arrest or denied the liberty to pursue any political or intellectual activity. Many distinguished Filipinos managed to leave the country, but those who could not leave lived in mental anguish, kept alert only by hope for the return of freedom. The helplessness of any individual who was out of favor with the regime either destroyed his spirit and weakened his will or it aroused savage hatred that festered within. Although all expression of protest was forbidden, the Catholic hierarchy and the Protestant church leaders courageously and repeatedly denounced the flagrant violations of civil liberty. A new Christian left, led mainly by foreign Roman Catholic priests, organized and supported what little opposition there was to martial law. Some were deported for their activities. Some distinguished former political leaders, including President Macapagal, gave voice to their faith in the democratic process and an active underground managed to transmit some of its grievances to the outside world.

Internal Problems. This balance sheet is by no means definitive; it is simply too early to pass judgment on the record of the government's handling of its continuing social and political problems. Since the imposition of martial law, President Marcos has been free to determine how the needs of society should be balanced against the rights of the individual. He has acted on the belief that the plight of his nation demanded drastic measures regardless of human cost: national survival was at stake. Some of the results he has achieved have been spectacular, some questionable, and some painful. In the months ahead adjustments will have to be made if authority is to be maintained and tyranny avoided, law and order guaranteed, a measure of freedom restored, progress accelerated and revolution forestalled.

The actual extent of the achievements and problems of the Philippine government under martial law cannot be determined with precision from the outside. With the disappearance of the free press, relatives and friends of President Marcos acquired newspapers and radio and television stations and the media became instruments of propaganda or dull house organs of the administration. Little reliable information was released about the state of affairs either at home or abroad, and government press handouts were orchestrated to indicate the persistence of conditions that made the police state necessary.

The government denied the existence of censorship but set up an Advisory Council to establish guidelines for the media. These guidelines, forty-five pages of rules and directives, provided that among other things no articles could be printed to discredit the government or to provoke discontent, due respect must be shown for the president and his office, and no discussion of the president, his integrity, the issues involved in the New Society, or the success or possible duration of martial law could be printed or broadcast. Even rumor mongering could be interpreted as a threat to national security and a crime against the state. The public was nurtured on the dangers of subversion, insurgency, and communism: stories of Communist infiltration into labor unions and student organizations multiplied while commentaries on foreign policy invariably endorsed various aspects of the New Developmental Diplomacy. The true situation in Luzon, the Visayas, or the Muslim south could never be determined by a study of official communiqués.

One of President Marcos's genuine achievements was the restoration of law and order in areas under government control. Marcos gave the people a new sense of security. He abolished the rule of guns and goons and he made the streets of Manila as safe as any in Asia. He reduced crimes of violence and kept reports of those that still occurred out of the papers. He imposed a curfew, clearing the streets at 1 a.m., and outside of Manila, except in the areas under rebel control, he restored the feeling that it was possible to travel without danger to life and limb.

Marcos inherited an insurgency situation that was potentially grave. After the arrest of the Communist leaders under Magsaysay and the formal outlawing of the Philippine Communist party in 1957, the activities of the People's Liberation Army (successors to the Huks) amounted to nothing more than brigandage and extortion. Early in 1960 new leftist, antigovernment movements with anti-American overtones developed in student, journalistic, labor, and even some business circles. As radicalism increased, such front organizations as the National Youth Movement and the Free Peasants Union appeared and the Communist party of the Philippines tried to revitalize itself. A pro-Moscow group limited itself to mild opposition to the government and the unequal treaties with the United States, while a more radical faction formed a new Communist party of the Philippines-Marxist Leninist, more commonly referred to as the Communist party of the Philippines-Mao Tse-tung Thought or "Maoists" for short. This faction formed the New People's Army (NPA) in 1969 and launched a campaign of terrorism in the countryside and the cities to bring down the government.[40]

Marcos claimed that by the time of martial law, the Maoists had established communal farms and production bases in the large segment of northeast Luzon under their control. They received little if any money or support from Mao Tse-tung and were Maoist only in the sense that they were fanatical in struggling for revolution. They organized the peasantry, as Mao had done in his youth, and they formed a broad united front with students and the proletariat in the urban centers. According to Marcos, Maoists could place as many as 1,800 guerrilla fighters in the field on all fronts with some 20,000 to 25,000 local supporters. Skirmishes between the NPA and the government forces took a heavy toll of civilians. Soon after the declaration of martial law, Marcos decimated the ranks of the NPA and captured most of their best-known leaders. Recognizing that any ideological movement might develop into a full-blown rebellion, he nevertheless expressed his confidence at the end of 1976 that the remnants of the NPA were receiving no help whatsoever from the outside and that the only remaining threat to internal security was the state of the national health.[41]

The president was less successful in achieving a satisfactory solution for the problems of the 3 million member Muslim minority in Mindanao, the Sulu Archipelago, Basilan, Tawi Tawi, and Palawan.[42] This community, although fragmented by ethnic and tribal loyalties, was united in its opposition to Marcos, its discontent fanned by Filipino Christian immigration from Luzon into Muslim areas and by

---

[40] Justus M. Van de Kroef, "The Philippines," in *Yearbook on International Communist Affairs* (Stanford: Hoover Institution Press, 1976), pp. 359-371.
[41] *U.S. News and World Report*, November 22, 1976, p. 65.
[42] Lela G. Noble, "The Moro National Liberation Front," a paper delivered for the 1976 annual meeting of the Association for Asian Studies, Toronto, Canada, March 1976. The author is also indebted to Ms. Noble for her annual summaries on the Philippines in *The Asian Survey*.

the failure of the Manila government to improve social, political, and economic conditions in Mindanao. In 1968 the lines of conflict were sharply drawn when some thirty Muslim soldiers in the national armed forces being trained on Corregidor Island for infiltration into Sabah, a Muslim part of North Borneo belonging to Malaysia but claimed by the Philippines, mutinied and were shot by their Filipino (Christian) officers. One of the repercussions of this incident was the formation of the Muslim Independence Movement in Mindanao. The independence movement organization was dissolved by the government, but its leaders, reinforced by young, active Muslim intellectuals, formed the Moro National Liberation Front (MNLF) in 1970. The MNLF, based at Mindanao State University at Marawi City, denounced the rule of the Filipino Christian administration and demanded autonomy for the Muslim regions. In addition, it dedicated itself to the promotion of Muslim culture and prepared for effective military action. The MNLF obtained supplies, arms, and ammunition from neighboring Sabah and enjoyed the sympathy and support of the Muslim states in Southeast Asia and the Middle East, especially Libya. When President Marcos, at the proclamation of martial law, ordered the Muslims to turn in their arms, he precipitated rebellion among tribesmen who, it is said, would sooner give up their wives than their guns.[43]

The level of violence increased, and in October 1972 the Muslims attacked Marawi City and conducted forays in parts of Lanao, Cotabato, Zamboanga, and Sulu. The government was taken by surprise and was not able to defeat the Muslim rebels although it engaged some 30,000 regular troops in addition to about 30,000 members of the constabulary, roughly 40 percent of the country's total military strength. The government suffered 7,000 or 8,000 casualties and reportedly lost most of the 1973 graduates of the Philippine Military Academy killed in action. Thereupon, Marcos undertook the organization of local civil defense forces to help him in Mindanao and held out various olive branches while he conducted military operations. He offered amnesty to rebels who would surrender, appointed Muslim local government officials for Muslim areas, offered more local autonomy, and increased the central government's subsidies for roads, schools, and public health. He conducted intermittent peace conferences with Muslim leaders at home and abroad and took advantage of personal schisms between the Muslim leaders themselves. Declaring

---

[43] Sydney Schanberg, *New York Times*, March 26, 1974.

that the old-style corrupt sultans would have to go, Marcos vowed that he would deal only with leaders of integrity and high morality.[44] Six lesser dignitaries of the front, led by Abdul Hamid Lukman, a former judge in Sulu, were invited to come to Manila in 1975 to negotiate a cease-fire. The president agreed to pull his regular troops out of the area while Lukman promised to try to persuade his colleagues to accept the government's program of greater autonomy without secession. While Lukman preempted the spotlight, the real leader of the front, Nur Misuari, a young ex-student radical, retired to Libya where he announced that he regarded the cease-fire as a stratagem to deceive and divide his people and vowed to continue to fight until all his demands were met.

While peace maneuvering was in progress, the fighting continued. As many as 100,000 government troops including the home defense forces were tied down and government costs reached an estimated $275,000 per day. Civilian deaths in Mindanao approached the 10,000 mark and more than 500,000 were made homeless. Although so many Muslim soldiers surrendered that the government began to suspect a plot (26,000 according to government figures) the rebels managed to maintain a fighting force estimated to be between 12,000 and 30,000 with substantial numbers of hard-core guerrillas some of whom had received training abroad. These soldiers were uniformed and well armed and their operations included hijacking government vessels and an airplane and engaging in skirmishes with government patrols. They were reported to have Soviet-made AK-47s imported from Sabah, Indonesia, Vietnam, or the Middle East; American-made antitank guns and M-16s captured, stolen, or bought from the Philippine army; and French-made mortars, as was proved in the bombardment of Cotabato City. The fighting—which amounted to civil war—had been fierce, with atrocities on both sides. By 1975 the rebels had gained control of the countryside in six provinces, seized and destroyed towns, and infiltrated or bombarded large cities. The government forces had been forced to abandon their defensive positions in the cities and sweep out into the countryside against the rebels, using artillery, cannons, and F-5s in the air to pound their strongholds.[45]

---

[44] Tom Weber, interview with President Marcos, *San Francisco Chronicle*, October 16 and 17, 1976.
[45] Bernard Wideman, "Stepping Up Terror in Mindanao," *Far Eastern Economic Review*, October 10, 1975.

Realizing the danger of the rebellion's turning into a holy war and fearing a cut-off of Arab oil, Marcos invited outside participation in the search for a negotiated settlement. The foreign ministers of Libya, Saudi Arabia, Senegal, and Somalia, representing the Secretariat of the Islamic Conference, held discussions with representatives of the Philippine government and in 1975 sent a mission to look into conditions in the Southern Philippines. Through the good offices of Colonel Qaddafi and with the participation of the representatives of the quadripartite Arab ministerial commission, the Philippine government and the MNLF reached an agreement for a cease-fire to be effective December 24, 1976. This agreement, according to published reports, provided for autonomy, but not secession or independence, for a region comprising thirteen provinces with a total population of 6 million; Muslim participation in the defense forces of the region and in the central government of the Philippines; a new bank for the development of the Muslim areas; Muslim control of local courts, schools, colleges, and administration; and formal recognition by the Manila government that an Islamic society and way of life existed in the south.[46]

A plebiscite was proposed to determine the future of the region but neither Marcos nor the MNLF could agree on specifications. Marcos wanted a plebiscite for the entire region of thirteen provinces as a precondition for autonomy but the MNLF objected since Christians outnumbered Muslims two to one in the entire region. Muslims enjoyed an absolute majority in only five or six of the provinces and their loyalties were divided between the MNLF and the newly created Muslim Reform Liberation Movement sponsored by Manila and headed by Lukman. The MNLF was not eager for a showdown at the polls and intensified its preparations for a new round of fighting. Mrs. Marcos journeyed again to Libya where she worked out a new formula for preserving the peace with Colonel Qaddafi and the Islamic Conference. In accordance with its terms, Marcos unilaterally proclaimed autonomy for the thirteen provinces on March 28, 1977 and announced that he would set up a provisional government for the region which would be subject to a popular referendum. These moves offended those Filipinos who opposed any possible separatism in their country and feared for the welfare of Christians under a Muslim regime. They did not allay the misgivings of non-MNLF Muslims in the affected area and fell far short of the extreme MNLF demands for a separate state with its own

---

[46] *Philippine News*, San Francisco, February 5-11, 1977.

78

name, flag, seal, security forces, courts, power of taxation, and Arabic language.[47]

From time to time Marcos has implied that the NPA exerted Communist influence on the MNLF, but the front denies this. Some Muslim leaders, including Nur Misuari himself, have disavowed their own Communist or at least radical backgrounds in the belief that godless communism was incompatible with their faith in God. Their religious convictions are anathema to Communists. Nevertheless, some NPA activists belonging to such Socialist-inclined groups as the Federations of Free Farmers have apparently taken advantage of the opportunity to cooperate with the Muslims in opposing the government. Rebel casualties have included well-known NPA leaders. The radicalism of the MNLF leadership stems from the bitterness of its experience, but its ideology is rooted in its Muslim culture rather than in any penchant for revolution.

The struggle in the southern Philippines, essentially sectarian, has economic roots that go very deep. The Muslim provinces are rich in rice, rubber, coconuts, pineapples, bananas, and minerals. The immigrant Christian farmers have acquired title to much of the best land throughout the region and together with foreign investors have developed large and prosperous plantations. Non-Muslim businessmen, largely from Luzon and Cebu, dominate the financial and commercial sectors. The Muslims have no love for the Christian missionaries and educators who have come along with the businessmen. The resources of Mindanao have enormous potential for the national development of the Philippines and the Muslims want their share of the profits. Most ordinary Muslims are not aware of the competition for their natural resources, but the Muslim leaders are, and they want control of whatever oil is to be found under the Sulu Sea.

As destruction and death continue, the hatreds burn deeper. No end is in sight and the future depends upon the government's strength, its ability to win the hearts and minds of local people, and its success in preventing too much outside help from reaching the rebels.

It must be repeated that our information about conditions inside the Philippines is incomplete. The press in the Philippines does not report the exact nature and extent of the fighting nor the progress of

[47] Rodney Tasker, "The Moro Rebellion," *Far Eastern Economic Review*, January 14, 1977; "Marcos Peace Maneuvers," ibid., January 28, 1977; "Peace or Plebiscite Choice for Marcos," ibid., March 18, 1977; and "Imelda Tries To Keep the Peace," ibid., April 1, 1977.

negotiations. Government press releases are confusing, being optimistic or gloomy depending on the government's interests. Only limited access to the area is granted to foreign travelers, scholars, and correspondents and their reports are subject to subtle forms of censorship. It is difficult to assess with certainty the claims which President Marcos makes in his dealings with the rebels.

Some other aspects of the internal situation in the Philippines were barred from open discussion because they tended to reveal flaws in the armor of the president. As time passed, the standards of public service under martial law began to slip and the armed forces stepped beyond the limits of their ordinary functions to assume police and intelligence responsibilities. As their numbers grew after 1972 the quality and morale of the government forces began to deteriorate and their fighting record in Mindanao and Luzon was blemished by widespread tales of incompetence and cruelty.

The constabulary or armed police seems to have degenerated even faster than the regular army. Reports of bribery multiplied between 1972 and 1977 and in some areas of the Visayas the rule of the constabulary was described as a veritable cesspool. In the bureaucracy, too, many of the old careless habits returned. Even in the first blush of martial law, the new bureaucrats had not been entirely above reproach and the enthusiasm of the early days quickly gave way to overconfidence and complacency. Transactions with the post-martial law police, customs authorities, magistrates, tax collectors, and postmasters were carried on, as usual, under the table. Instead of being eliminated, corruption took new forms. Late in 1975 thousands of government functionaries, including the president's executive secretary, men of cabinet rank, the commissioners of the budget, the customs, and internal revenue were dismissed, and lesser purges were continuous both in the civil service and the ranks of the military.[48] The tensions were so great that in October one of President Marcos's most trusted assistants was slain in his own office.

The most controversial question to plague the nation was the integrity of the president and his family. Though he talked much of

---

[48] Bernard Wideman, "Politics of the Purge," *Far Eastern Economic Review,* October 31, 1975, p. 10, describes the purge of 2,664 officials and civil servants up to the cabinet level for irregularities. This purge produced bitter in-fighting in the president's official family. As a result, Executive Secretary Alejandro Melchor, one of the most capable men in the government, lost his job. Apparently he had aroused the ire of Mrs. Marcos and the secretary of national defense.

character, Marcos was ruthless in dealing with friends and enemies alike. He spoke of love for the masses but made no headway in identifying himself with them; he professed sympathy with the poor but was notorious for his wealth; while he asked his people to accept austerity, he indulged his taste for ostentatious living. Cautiously referred to as Mr. Ten Percent, the president did not hesitate to put financial screws on ex-oligarchs of both parties.

The first lady, meanwhile, although a person of great charm and intelligence, was caustically criticized for her acquisitiveness and extravagance. No actress ever attracted more publicity, no socialite commanded more attention. Imperious as a queen, she felt her people understood and responded to her grand manner. When she gave orders, there was no need for the president's counter-signature. On November 6, 1975, Mrs. Marcos was sworn in as governor of the metropolitan Manila area, a position second in importance only to that of her husband.

In her unofficial capacity, Mrs. Marcos achieved notoriety as the most glamorous of the international jet set. Her travels took her to Moscow and Peking, Tehran and Cairo, Lima, Mexico City, and Havana. Her parties became the scandal of Manila. Her staging of the Miss Universe pageant, her descent on the coronation ceremonies of the King of Nepal, her appearance at the opening of the Sydney Opera House were straight Hollywood. When a former chairman of the Media Advisory Council defected to the United States in 1975, he said his action was prompted by scandals that made Watergate look trivial.[49]

If the credibility of the Marcos regime was subject to question, nevertheless disapproval of the personal conduct of the president and his family could not be openly expressed. The speeches and books of the president about the democratic revolution packed little popular appeal, and martial law as a revolutionary process smacked more of repression than of progress. *Barangay* democracy, appointed legislative assemblies, and popular referenda were looked upon as little more than subtle methods of mass manipulation. Nobody shed tears for the

---

[49] U.S. Congress, House of Representatives, *Hearings on Human Rights*, pp. 465-480. A memorandum submitted by Primitivo Mijares, June 17, 1975, gives the details of his bitter case against President and Mrs. Marcos. Mijares interprets the farewell to democracy and the rise of the conjugal dictatorship as a carefully conceived and well-executed plot. These charges were branded as unfounded by the solicitor general of the Philippines. See pages 421-423 of the *Hearings*.

passing of the graft-ridden election process or the late influence-peddling Congress, but a good many Filipinos retained some faith in democracy as an ideal in spite of its past failures in the Philippines.

Much of the success that Marcos claimed for his administration under martial law could reasonably be attributed to the values underlying Philippine society. Although on the eve of martial law a great number of Filipinos were demanding change, the majority had shied away from revolution. The president had sensed their mood and responded to it. It was not difficult to enforce discipline in a society where a family system with a deep respect for kinship obligations, a common religion, and confidence in mass education, individual liberty, and social mobility still prevailed. President Marcos fashioned a regime that, while it violated many of the principles upon which recent political experience in the Philippines had been predicated, conformed to the basic Filipino demand for progress within the rule of law. His future would depend upon his ability to keep the reins tight, yet sufficiently adjustable to accommodate gradually the popular desire for greater freedom. From time to time he relaxed his rule; alternately he tightened his grip. He made a show of releasing prisoners in accordance with his announced policy of reconciliation, solidarity, and brotherhood —meanwhile purging thousands of bureaucrats whom he denounced for wrongdoing.

Marcos made no promises as to when or how martial law would end, though he told his people that he had worked out a plan for the orderly transfer of the reins of government in the event of his death. It was rumored that he had provided for a junta, or council, composed primarily of military men but headed by Mrs. Marcos. A master manipulator, Marcos attuned his demands upon the nation to his sense of the popular mood.

The people could not help growing increasingly restive under martial law. The men of the church were divided between those who were content to pray and those who participated in protest. The Philippine Civil Liberties Union circulated a mimeographed appeal for elections to a National Assembly as provided by the new but suspended constitution. This circular said that the situation was now so grave that it could be remedied only through the concerted effort of all Filipinos and contended that people have a right to civil disobedience if denied their due. Former political leaders like Senators Diokno, Tolentino, Salonga, and Tanada and former President Macapagal, aired their views in defiance of martial law. One hundred thirty Filipinos, among them the respected Jesuit writer Horacio de la Costa, appealed to the nation to consider alternatives to both communism and the one-man rule of President Marcos. S. P. Lopez, a former Marcos spokesman, ambassador to the United States, and president of the University of the Philippines, rejected as untenable the claim that after four years martial law was still necessary for social reform.[50]

It was significant that President Marcos could neither indicate when martial law would end nor tolerate any expression of opposition. His control over the affairs of the Philippines, both domestic and foreign was complete.

Foreign Affairs. The period of martial law in the Philippines coincided with great diplomatic changes in the Western Pacific. Japan, the People's Republic of China, the U.S.S.R., and the countries of Western Europe were assuming new roles in the shaping of a power equilibrium in East and Southeast Asia. Martial law gave President Marcos and Secretary Romulo much-needed room to maneuver in defining the interests and carrying out the policies of the Philippines. The collapse of the American effort and the Communist takeover in Indochina accentuated trends that had already been discernible in Philippine strategy and tactics. On May 23, 1975, President Marcos announced his guidelines for action:

> First, to intensify, along a broader field, our relations with the members of ASEAN. . . . Second, to pursue more vigorously the establishment of diplomatic relations with socialist states, in particular with the People's Republic of China and with the Soviet Union. . . . Third, to seek closer identification with the Third World with whom we share similar problems. . . . Fourth, to continue our beneficial relationship with Japan. . . . Fifth, to support the Arab countries in their struggle for a just and enduring peace in the Middle East. . . . Finally, to find a new basis compatible with the emerging realities in Asia for a continuing healthy relationship with the United States.[51]

---

[50] For information on conditions as they developed, the author followed carefully the *New York Times, Far Eastern Economic Review,* the *Philippine News* (San Francisco), the *Asian Survey* (Berkeley: University of California) and the annual *Asia Yearbook* (Hong Kong: Far Eastern Economic Review).

[51] Text released May 23, 1975, by the Office of the President, Manila. See also Peter Bathurst, "New Directions for the New Society," *Far Eastern Economic Review,* insert section entitled, "Focus on the Philippines," June 13, 1975, p. 3.

The Philippines made a strong pitch for influence in Asia. President Marcos repeatedly stressed the fact that he was an Asian in order to bolster his personal image and bargaining position and professed faith in Asian ideals of compassion and spiritual freedom. Gandhi, Buddha, and Christ he claimed as his fellow Asians. The Asian mission, Marcos believed, was to combine spiritual maturity with the Western qualities of political stability and economic prosperity.

Looking to the major Asian powers, Marcos continued to try to attract as much Japanese trade and investment as possible to the Philippines. Cooperation, he believed, was the best way to prevent the militarization of Japan and to put a limit on Japanese economic expansion on the Asian continent. He did not trust the Japanese, but he preferred a three-way interdependency between the Philippines, Japan, and the United States to a situation where both the Philippines and Japan were little more than American satellites. After the ratification on December 21, 1973, of the Treaty of Amity, Commerce and Navigation with Japan, the Philippines welcomed substantial Japanese investment in a steel plant, a petrochemical complex, a wood-processing plant, and new sugar centrals. Mutual profits tended to make the Philippines forget its bitter memories of World War II, but Marcos himself suggested that ASEAN would be well advised to seek economic and security pacts with Japan guaranteeing that a rearmed Japan would not again become a predatory power.

A bold step in the pursuit of détente with the People's Republic of China was the visit to Peking by the first lady in September 1974. Mrs. Marcos had interviews with Chou En-lai and Mao Tse-tung and, disregarding the insurgents at home, hailed Mao as one of the greatest leaders in history. She concluded a trade agreement that provided for the exchange of Chinese petroleum products for copra, lumber, sugar, copper, and other metals from the Philippines. At the risk of antagonizing Taiwan and losing the support of the anti-Communist Chinese in the Philippines, she laid the groundwork for an official visit by the president himself in June 1975.[52] On that visit, President Marcos declared that he had set his mind at rest about the role of Peking in the Communist resistance in the Philippines. He, too, saluted Mao as a natural leader of the Third World, and in accord with the Philippine policy of opening windows to the outside world, abrogated

[52] *Asia Yearbook*, 1975, p. 262, and *Peking Review*, October 4, 1974, p. 5.

all treaties and agreements between the Philippines and Taiwan and established normal relations with Peking. [53]

In its relations with Japan and China, the Philippines had less leeway than it had in Southeast Asia, where it felt that it was dealing with equals. The Philippines was not willing to abandon its claim to Sabah, but pushed the dispute into the background in the interest of a better understanding with Malaysia. Complete friendship, on the other hand, was impossible as long as Malaysia was suspected of supporting the Muslim rebels in Mindanao and Sulu. In 1974 both Mrs. Marcos and President Marcos visited Indonesia and took every opportunity to associate their nation more closely with the thriving Indonesia that had arisen after Sukarno. At successive conferences on the law of the sea, the Philippines supported the Indonesian archipelago doctrine, which held that waters within the extreme boundaries of island states should be considered territorial waters. This doctrine was vital to states that entertained high hopes for the petroleum reserves that might be discovered in off-shore fields.

With the withdrawal of the Philippine forces from Vietnam and the reduction of the American military presence in Southeast Asia, the Philippines jockeyed for a position of greater leadership in regional development. It argued for the strengthening of ASEAN and the Asia Development Bank, and President Marcos proposed the establishment of an Asian forum for the settlement of Asian issues, including the rehabilitation of Indochina and Asia's role in an egalitarian world order. Malaysia proposed, and the Philippines enthusiastically endorsed, the principle that Asia should become a zone of peace, freedom, and neutrality.

The Philippines made itself the spokesman for the smaller Asian nations that were determined never again to be pawns in the life and death game of great-power politics. Speaking in Bangkok in 1974, Secretary Romulo warned against the fight for influence between the superpowers and urged Southeast Asians to be watchful and to combine their strength so as not to be mesmerized or pushed aside by Kissinger

---

[53] *Peking Review,* June 13, 1975, pp. 3-8. *New York Times,* June 10, 1975, p. 3; June 12, 1975, p. 6; and June 15, 1975, section 4, p. 4. The *New York Times,* October 14, 1975, p. 2 says that the People's Republic of China took over the Chinese Embassy in Manila and some Taiwan diplomats who had left Manila in June returned to set up a Pacific Commercial and Cultural Center as a Manila-Taipei Liaison Office.

or his successor in whatever schemes might be put forth for a new balance of power in Asia. In 1976 the Philippines was not accepted as an observer at the Colombo conference of the nonaligned powers but it was awarded guest status and it was the prime mover in pushing the ASEAN members beyond economic cooperation toward political togetherness. Both Marcoses attended the UNCTAD meetings in Nairobi and agreed to host the UNCTAD meetings in Manila in 1979.[54]

The Philippines did not panic at the Communist victories in Indochina. Some Philippine political commentators stressed the fact that many Americans had had their doubts about Vietnam from the beginning and labeled the withdrawal an exercise of the collective American conscience. The outcome in Vietnam, according to them, was not the result of American weakness or a harbinger of neo-isolationism in the United States but a product of the suffering caused by the long war and the determination of the North Vietnamese to reunite their nation. Very few sophisticated Filipinos feared that the Philippines would be the next domino to fall. Instead they had faith that their own country and its anti-Communist neighbors had become sufficiently strong to assert their independence from the West and adopt a wide, nonideological perspective in protecting their own interests.

The Philippines became the spokesman in ASEAN for the recognition of the new governments in Cambodia, Vietnam, and Laos and led the discussions for incorporating these states into the new regional organization. The Philippines bent over backwards to avoid giving offense to the Revolutionary Government of Vietnam in the matter of refugees, and, though it permitted the entry of evacuees on the way to the United States, gave warning that it would arrest any military and/or civilian officials of the former South Vietnamese regime who set foot on Philippine soil. In fact, no arrests were made but no South Vietnamese leaders were granted asylum in the Philippines. The Philippine government, in extraordinarily considerate language, expressed its desire to keep its channels of communication open to Hanoi. North Vietnam was conspicuously added to the list of Socialist countries with which the Philippines desired broader relations, and

---

[54] See *Bangkok Post*, August 15, 1974, p. 1, Far Eastern Economic Review, *Asia Yearbook, 1977*, p. 58 ff., and Lela Noble, "Philippines 1976: The Contrast between Shrine and Shanty," *Asian Survey*, February 1977, pp. 133-142.

when Vietnam announced its unification, the Philippines was among the first to extend recognition.[55]

Looking beyond Asia, the Philippines sought wider contacts in Western Europe, Eastern Europe, Latin America, and the Middle East. Mrs. Marcos visited Moscow in 1971, touching off rumors of diplomatic recognition, and Secretary Romulo suddenly became the roving champion of peaceful coexistence. The Philippines already recognized Yugoslavia and Rumania; in the early 1970s normal diplomatic relations were extended to East Germany, Poland, Czechoslovakia, Hungary, Bulgaria, and Mongolia. But the most startling development occurred in relations with the Soviet Union. In September 1974 Marcos declared his support for wider cultural cooperation with the U.S.S.R. and concluded an agreement providing for exchange of scholars, tourists, and sports groups. Festivals, symposiums, lectures, and exhibitions were scheduled to be held under the agreement. In response, the Soviet government commended him for reform and condemned the splinter groups, deriving their inspiration from Mao, who stooped to terrorism and discredited the progressive forces in the Philippines. The two countries agreed to normalize diplomatic relations in May 1976.[56]

The Philippines paid unusual attention to Latin America. Taking advantage of her Spanish-Catholic heritage, Mrs. Marcos undertook a good-will mission to Mexico, Venezuela and Bolivia. In August 1975, she visited Cuba, where she and Castro issued a joint statement calling for the restoration of diplomatic relations. [57] Mrs. Marcos also carried out successful diplomatic missions to Egypt, Saudi Arabia, and Libya, paving the way for Arab cooperation in matters of oil, capital investments, and the Muslim insurgency. The Philippines could not afford to follow the American lead in Arab-Israeli relations and considered diplomatic courtesy the least price it could expect to pay for precious Middle Eastern oil. Marcos not only wanted Arab support for him-

[55] On August 7, 1975, the deputy foreign minister of North Vietnam announced that a joint communiqué had been signed in Hanoi establishing relations between North Vietnam and the Philippines at the ambassadorial level. It was claimed that as one of the terms the Philippines agreed not to allow any foreign country to use Philippine territory as a base for direct or indirect aggression against any country in the region. Harvey Stockwin, in the *Far Eastern Economic Review*, December 12, 1975, reported that, contrary to Hanoi's claim, the Philippines and North Vietnam had not yet agreed to establish normal diplomatic relations and no joint communiqué had been signed.

[56] *New York Times*, June 2, 1976, p. 15; June 3, 1976, p. 40.

[57] *New York Times*, August 28, 1975, p. 7, and *Far Eastern Economic Review*, September 12, 1975, p. 50.

self but also wanted to make sure that his Muslim foes would not receive money, supplies, and arms from their Arab coreligionists.[58]

Relations with the United States

Under martial law, President Marcos exhibited the same tendencies and attitudes toward the United States that he had displayed in the first blush of his New Developmental Diplomacy. His statements and actions, together with the resulting political and psychological climate in the Philippines, had a profound effect in Washington. Although President Marcos listed Asia and the rest of the world first in his guidelines for foreign policy, he recognized the supreme importance of a continuing healthy relationship with the United States, especially after the fall of South Vietnam. For all his criticism of the United States and insistence on Philippine self-reliance, he took care to preserve the facade of close ties and good will.

After the American withdrawal from Indochina, the Filipinos had to reckon with the possibility that the United States might, in a mood of frustration, pull its remaining military forces out of Southeast Asia, give up its bases, and reduce its commitments to the Philippines. They also contemplated the more pleasant alternative, that after Vietnam the Philippines might become more important rather than less important in the forward strategy of the United States. If this were the case, the Americans would be willing to pay more rather than less for Philippine cooperation. The Philippine leaders had no intention of letting themselves be relegated to the status of pawns in the game of American power politics. They were determined not to be taken lightly as the United States searched for a new role in Southeast Asia. The Philippines would have to be compensated handsomely for whatever of value it might contribute to the United States. The challenge was to discover the combination of gestures and attitudes that would bring the Philippines the greatest return and best promote its national interests.

Problems of Mutual Security. The first problems to command the attention of President Marcos were those engendered by the inadequacies of the Mutual Defense Treaty and of such peripheral commitments as had been made by various presidents, secretaries of state,

---

[58] Rodney Tasker, "The Moro Rebellion," *Far Eastern Economic Review*, January 14, 1977.

and ambassadors. As American embarrassments in Indochina escalated, the Filipinos became increasingly disturbed by the knowledge that statements made by Americans in the executive branch of government were commitments only of the administration in power, mere declarations of intent without binding effect on the people or the Congress. In his speech of May 23, 1975, Marcos said: "It is difficult if not impossible to stake the nation's survival on whimsical interpretations of the mutual defense agreements which are apparently dependent not on legal commitments but on the mood of the nation in any given historical period." [59] Philippine lawyers and diplomats were aware of the constitutional limitations on the American executive, but the debate in the U.S. Congress on war powers aroused new fears that the Philippines might become disastrously involved in American conflicts and that in a crunch the Americans might desert the Philippines just as they had Vietnam. Although many Filipinos clung to their confidence in the United States and in the sincerity of American intentions, they were forced to recognize that, in the prevailing American political climate, all foreign commitments including those to the Philippines would be subject to the strictest construction.

President Marcos assured President Ford on the latter's succession to office that he would find in the Philippines a dependable and firm ally, one that shared the United States's desire to build a world without war, poverty, illiteracy, disease, and human exploitation. Marcos expressed his satisfaction that Ford intended to continue on the course set by his predecessor and promised that no deviations would occur on his own part to erode U.S.-Philippine relations.[60] But the enormity of the American collapse in Vietnam in April 1975 strengthened his conviction that he would have to reexamine the entire security relationship with the United States.

President Marcos wanted the U.S. bases in the Philippines to be known henceforth as Philippine bases. The existence of "American" bases on Philippine soil was an affront to national pride and dignity, a vestige of the hated extraterritorial system, and a denial of Philippine sovereignty. Worse, the bases had become of questionable value to the Philippines. The U.S. military presence in the Philippines could not help Marcos in his fight against insurgents—he could never be

---

[59] *Far Eastern Economic Review*, June 13, 1975, p. 9.
[60] The White House released the exchange of notes between Presidents Marcos and Ford on August 9, 1974.

sure that the Americans would come to his help, and in any case he could not wait for them. In view of the unpredictability of the American Congress, he could never count on American military action on his behalf. He was inclined to feel that the presence of the bases would only embarrass him in his relations with ASEAN and the Socialist world and might conceivably serve as a pretext for an attack on the Philippines from the outside.

He had other doubts about the bases, too. Their economic value would go down if the level of American military activity declined. Reductions in American force levels might result from American budget stringencies or the force of public opinion, or they might be dictated by a strategy of Europe First. Above all, Filipinos did not want to be caught in the middle of a nuclear war, and they feared that the likelihood of nuclear attack was greatest wherever Americans were stationed. Marcos reasoned that if the bases were no longer needed by the United States, they could serve no useful purpose either for the Philippines or the United States. On the contrary, they would be a liability to both parties, a drain on American reserves on the one hand and on the other a source of international tensions in Asia that could provoke unwarranted aggression against the Philippines.[61]

Although the bases agreement was supposed to run until 1991, President Marcos asked that negotiations for modifications be undertaken as expeditiously as possible. He did not want to review the entire agreement, only such clauses as he found objectionable, and instead of settling all existing problems, at a general conference he preferred to tackle issues one at a time, in secret, so as to derive maximum political and diplomatic advantage for himself. He did not demand the immediate or total withdrawal of the Americans since he valued their contributions to Philippine security and had no wish to destroy their capacity to operate efficiently in the Western Pacific. The U.S. presence was encouraged, he said, and all the leaders of Asia agreed that it would be impossible to maintain peace in the area without it.[62] But Marcos believed the time had come to consider seriously the phasing out of American control of the bases under arrangements allowing him to contract with the Americans for the payment of rent at his pleasure. If the bases were Filipino rather than American, he could

61 *Far Eastern Economic Review*, June 13, 1975, p. 9.
62 *U.S. News and World Report*, November 22, 1976, p. 65. Interview with President Marcos.

rent them or develop them, with foreign help, for industrial purposes. The Japanese Kawasaki firm had indicated a desire to construct a shipyard at Subic Bay, which would be a boon to the Philippine economy. Furthermore, Marcos saw no reason why the facilities at the bases could not be made available to the Japanese, the Russians, or anyone else who wanted to use them. At the very least, Marcos wanted the absolute maximum in money for the use of the bases and demanded full legal jurisdiction over the 15,000 American servicemen stationed there.

Within the parameters laid down by President Marcos, discussions were undertaken in 1975 on such perennial sore spots as the expansion of Philippine jurisdictional and administrative rights, control of security, equal pay for equal work, nationality of the base commander, further reduction of base areas, payment of substantial rent by the United States, and reduction of the terms of the current leases from twenty-five to ten or even five years.

For the first time, the Philippines conducted the negotiations without attendant demonstrations and publicity aside from occasional articles in the government-controlled press. President Marcos was too shrewd to overlook the psychological benefits of a well-timed press release. Negotiations continued through 1976, sometimes in Washington and sometimes in the Philippines, without producing agreement. For the Philippines the issue of sovereignty was nonnegotiable; what had to be settled were the terms that would be acceptable for American use of Philippine bases and the sum of money in rent or aid that could be obtained in payment.

Marcos also considered a new understanding on military assistance essential to a healthy security relationship with the United States. In his public statements he was not disposed to acknowledge the huge amounts the Philippines had already received in U.S. military aid, preferring to stress the need to reassess the assistance agreements and eliminate their deficiencies. As he told President Ford, since it was his policy not to allow the introduction of ground troops into the Philippines except as a last resort and since the United States might not always be ready to come to his assistance, the Philippine Army itself must be prepared to meet all contingencies.[63] He felt that the

---

[63] James M. Naughton, *New York Times*, December 7, 1975.

Philippines was unjustly accused of trying to extort assistance from the United States and claimed that in many instances when he had been in great need, no aid had come. To fight the secessionists and insurgents, he said, he had had to buy arms from Singapore, Taiwan, and Europe because American help, agreed to and committed, either never arrived or arrived too late.[64] Marcos wanted the Americans to fulfill their promise to help him build up his capability to the point where Philippine forces could meet any threat to Philippine security with honor and dignity and without calling on foreign troops. As his troops broadened their field operations and the need for weapons and ammunition became critical, he demanded an end to the system of military handouts and its replacement by an assistance program geared toward Philippine self-reliance.

In an unusually frank public statement at the end of 1976, President Marcos said that he did not want blood money from the United States but only military supplies as already promised, under the Military Assistance Pact, as well as just rent in exchange for continued American use of Philippine bases. Marcos repeated that the Philippines must be self-reliant because there would be instances in the future when the United States would be prevented from coming to its defense by the inclinations and policies of the U.S. government itself. At the height of the Muslim rebellion when there was massive infiltration of material and men from outside the country, he recalled the United States had not been in a position to become involved. He remarked in conclusion that he anticipated no substantial change in Philippine-U.S. relations under the Carter administration and he definitely expected that the United States would try to anchor those relations in mutual trust, respect, and equality.[65]

Economic Relations. The Philippines faced the same dilemma in its economic relations with the United States that it encountered in the realm of national security: how to become self-reliant while still depending heavily on the United States. While President Marcos talked about self-reliance, however, he adopted policies that produced the opposite result. The Philippines wanted continuing economic aid, just as it wanted military aid, but there were limits to what it could persuade

---

[64] *U.S. News and World Report*, November 22, 1976, p. 65.
[65] *Agence France Presse,* Hong Kong, December 11, 1976, as reported in *Foreign Broadcast Information Service, Asia and the Pacific*, December 13, 1976.

the American government to give. The Philippines could only accept what the United States, and any other donors, including Japan and such international agencies as the World Bank and the Asia Development Bank, would make available in grants and loans.[66]

In seeking better relations with foreign business interests, as distinct from foreign governments, President Marcos endeavored to create an environment that would be attractive for private enterprise. Foreign capitalists were no longer castigated in the press as exploiters out to drain the life blood of the Philippines, but were hailed as entrepreneurs in search of fair and reasonable profits. At the time of the proclamation of martial law there were more Americans living and working in the Philippines than all other foreign nationals combined. American investments in private industry amounted to more than a billion dollars in book value (actual value may have been double that) and U.S. investments in government bonds were nearly as great. The American share in all foreign investments was 80 percent and growing, while in foreign trade it amounted to approximately one-third.[67] American capital and participation in development were needed to keep the Philippine economy going.

New regulations for foreign investments were promulgated after the declaration of martial law. Under these regulations, foreign firms were invited to take fullest advantage of Philippine labor, management skills, and familiarity with American business methods and the English language;[68] substantial inducements were offered to investors in new enterprises or enterprises that would contribute directly to national development or foreign trade; strikes were outlawed and minimum-wage regulations liberalized; restrictions were relaxed on land holding and

---

[66] See Raymond Cohen, "United States Aid," in *Development in the 70s* (Manila: U.S. Embassy, 1973), pp. 208-239 and John Hummon, "The Philippine-U.S. Relationship: Aid," in *The Philippine-American Relationship* (Manila: U.S. Embassy, 1974), pp. 151-161. These statements were made by officials in the Agency for International Development (AID), Manila, to annual seminars for student leaders conducted by the embassy.

[67] Information for this section was obtained from William E. Knight (U.S. Embassy, counselor for economic and commercial affairs), "Investment Issues and Philippine Economic Development," *Current Comment, Philippine-American Relations Series No. 12* (Manila: U.S. Embassy, no date). See also Terrell E. Arnold, "Current United States-Philippine Economic Relations," in *Development in the 70s*, pp. 237-265, and Armand V. Fabella and Terrell E. Arnold, "The Philippine-U.S. Relationship: Economics," in *The Philippine-American Relationship*, pp. 184-216.

[68] Tony Patrick, "Banking on the Marcos Method," *Far Eastern Economic Review*, September 27, 1974, pp. 67-69.

the entry of foreign capital into the extractive industries; the Americans were urged to take up the search for oil in the Philippines as they had done in Indonesia; foreign exchange rules were eased and repatriation of capital and profits was guaranteed; and multinational corporations were offered special incentives to make Manila their headquarters in Asia.[69]

As the actual accomplishments of national development dropped further behind the ambitious goals set by the government, the Philippines constantly changed the rules under which foreign capital could operate. More and more large companies were taken over by the Philippine government, including the Philippine National Oil Company (formerly ESSO Petroleum), the Luzon Stevedoring Company, and the National Electric Company. A new law forced firms with more than 500 employees to grow rice for their workers or buy it for them on the world market. Capital-participation regulations and management-labor relations were subject to continuous modification and spotty enforcement. Foreign investors responded cautiously to the new climate, inhibited by the whimsical behavior of the authoritarian regime. Foreign enterprise continued to be extremely profitable, but the inflow of capital was less than the Philippines had hoped for.

In trade President Marcos could not aspire to self-reliance, but he sought diversification that would further reduce Philippine dependence on the United States.[70] This accounted for frantic trade drives with Japan, the ASEAN countries, the rest of Asia, and the countries of Europe. With the expiration of the Laurel-Langley agreement in 1974, Marcos explored ways and means to preserve the benefits of special relations—that is, special privileges in the American market for favored products such as sugar, mahogany, and coconut oil—without surrendering compensating privileges for American products entering the Philippines. Any serious diminution in Philippine exports to the United States might have disastrous consequences for the Philippine economy, and hence for the Marcos regime. At the very least, therefore, the Filipinos wanted to win special concessions for themselves in spite of the Ameri-

---

[69] The regulations affecting investments from overseas are subject to constant change in response to current economic conditions. This analysis of the regulations in force at the time of writing was based on interviews with appropriate officials at the Central Bank of the Philippines, the American Chamber of Commerce, and the U.S. Embassy in Manila.

[70] Frank Golay, "The Philippine Relationship: Trade," in *The Philippine-American Relationship,* pp. 230-260.

can Trade Reform Act of 1974, which spelled doom for special preferences and extended generalized preferences to all underdeveloped countries. Marcos said he was not happy with the situation in which coconut oil, for instance, paid one cent a pound duty upon entering the United States, while competitive palm and vegetable oils paid none. He pointed out that Philippine mahogany paid double what other woods were charged in tariff duties and that the sugar trade of the Philippines was practically doomed with the loss of duty-free quotas.[71]

As long as the conditions of trade between the Philippines and the United States remained comparatively favorable to the Philippines—that is, as long as sugar prices remained firm—the Philippines was content to talk about reciprocity and equal treatment while seeking some kind of formula that would abandon the appearance but preserve the substance of special relations. Both the Philippines and the United States were casual about negotiating a Treaty of Amity and Commerce as long as trade without benefit of treaty continued to be mutually profitable. But anxiety returned when the bottom fell out of the sugar market and the spiralling price of imports, especially oil, aggravated the Philippines's negative balance of payments.

Preserving Good Will. Maneuvering to promote the interests of his country, President Marcos tried to minimize the psychological shock felt in the United States when he abandoned democracy. Their devotion to common ideals had been the strongest tie between the United States and the Philippines, and this tie was loosened by the imposition of martial law. Marcos went to unusual lengths to demonstrate his innate cordiality and desire to preserve the good will of the United States. More than anything he would have liked to win the outright approval of the United States, but he was at least gratified when the United States refrained from expressing official concern over his course. Under comparable circumstances in 1975, the United States had censured President Park of South Korea.

After the fall of Thieu in South Vietnam, Marcos argued that his personal success was essential for the attainment of the long-range goals of the United States in Southeast Asia: without him in Manila everything would fall to pieces. While he sought less dependence on the United States, he was careful to court a certain amount of American favor. He

[71] *U.S. News and World Report,* Interview with President Marcos, November 22, 1976, pp. 65-66.

did away with the blatant anti-Americanism of the fifties and sixties, but he tolerated (if he did not actually order) mild anti-Americanism in his own controlled press. Almost daily, columnists accused the United States of using the Philippines as a lackey, taking the Philippines for granted, or treating the Philippines with arrogance and insensitivity. The Filipinos were still reminded that it was the colonial mentality, nurtured by centuries of political, economic, and cultural subservience, that had made the resort to martial law necessary in the first place. The United States was chided for taking advantage of the Philippines economically and for failing to appreciate the sincerity and zeal of Marcos's commitment to the New Society.

President Marcos was obliged to compete with his own critics in seeking sympathy and support from the United States. Many of Marcos's most outspoken critics had been long identified as champions of democracy and friends of the United States, although they were as strongly nationalistic as Marcos had ever been. After martial law, they criticized the United States for going too far in support of Marcos and failing to take a stronger stand for the maintenance of American ideals in the Philippines. They clung to the hope that the United States would not be so blinded by its concern for security and its own strategic interests as to neglect its traditional concern for civil rights and representative government. They realized, however, that it was impolitic for the United States to seem to interfere in the internal affairs of the Philippines and that the accredited representatives of the United States would have to deal with the regime in power, whatever its nature.[72]

The opinions of private citizens in the Philippines about the United States after the setbacks in Indochina covered the spectrum from cynicism to sympathy. A well-known columnist, Teodoro Valencia, declared that the prestige of the United States in Southeast Asia and the Pacific had never sunk so low. "We shall remain friends with the United States," he wrote, "but such friendship must be based on her promise not to help us the way she helped Cambodia and Vietnam." A more charitable colleague of Valencia on the same paper, the *Bulletin Today*, insisted that Vietnam and Cambodia should be considered exceptions to

---

[72] Many of Marcos's critics took refuge in the United States and gave voice to their views in the House, *Hearings on Human Rights, 1975*. In such organizations as the Movement for a Free Philippines, the Union of Democratic Filipinos, and the National Committee for the Restoration of Civil Liberties, they urged the United States to withhold support for the Philippines as long as it was under martial law.

the general rule that the United States stands by its security arrangements.[73] These men were writing for publication, whereas articulate Filipinos in the privacy of their own homes seemed little disposed to doubt America's credibility because of Vietnam. Insofar as generalization is possible, Filipinos appreciated the anomalies of the situation into which the United States had been plunged and were not inclined to cast aside their faith in the purposes and intentions of the United States. No better evidence of Filipino good will could be found than the number of visitors and emigrants who swarmed into the American Embassy in Manila every day in quest of visas for the United States.

When President Ford visited the Philippines, he was given what Romulo called "the greatest reception given to any visitor to these islands." [74] Crowds lined the seven-mile parade route from the Manila airport to the presidential palace—but anti-Marcos priests, nuns, students, and workers were excluded from the carefully rehearsed demonstration. This official display of good feeling seemed to indicate that Marcos would continue to look to the United States for understanding and cooperation despite the strains that had arisen from martial law and might be aggravated by continuing conflicts of policy.

If President Marcos was perturbed by the concern for human rights that Jimmy Carter repeatedly expressed before entering the White House, he gave no public indication of his feelings. It was assumed that he would negotiate with Carter as he had with Carter's predecessors, relying on the mutuality of interests to enable him to retain the American commitment to Philippine security and American good will while seeking to reach the most advantageous arrangement possible on the use of his military bases, continuance of American military and economic assistance, and the promotion of Philippine trade.

---

[73] *New York Times,* April 13, 1975, p. 19.
[74] Ibid., December 7, 1975.

3

The United States and the Philippines: Pacific Doctrine and Future Policy

The adoption of President Marcos's New Developmental Diplomacy and the subsequent establishment of martial law formed the background against which successive American presidents—Johnson, Nixon, Ford, and Carter—were obliged to conduct their continuous reappraisal of the interests and policies of the United States in Asia, including the Philippines. Before Vietnam it was always assumed that the United States and the Philippines were dedicated to such common objectives as the containment of Communist aggression and the preservation of a democratic way of life, but after Vietnam this could not be taken for granted. As the Philippines became increasingly insistent on its independence, especially vis-à-vis the United States, it became necessary for Americans to reconsider whether the Philippines truly shared the historic ideals of the United States and to reassess the extent to which the tangible interests of the two countries coincided. This process of continuous reexamination brought forth repeated pronouncements of American doctrine with respect to Asia and the Pacific, including the Philippines, that were intended to set forth the guidelines for U.S. policies on mutual defense, maintenance of American bases and force levels, military and economic assistance, economic relations, and the preservation of good will in spite of disagreements over martial law and human rights.

Moral Commitment and the Concern for Credibility

As the fate of the Americans in Vietnam closed in, the United States sought to convince the world that it was as deeply committed as ever to the ideals and objectives that had prompted its intervention in Vietnam in the first place. The abandonment of its military effort by no means implied the surrender of its principles. To discharge the responsibilities of leadership that seemed to flow from American power, it was deemed essential to preserve the faith of America's friends and allies. Statements of policy intended to show the undiminished determination of the United States to stand by its commitments regardless of the blows of Indochina seemed, therefore, in order.

President Johnson's announcement in March 1968 that he would not run for reelection was the first signal of the need for new policies in Asia. The Tet offensive might have been a military victory for the American side, but it also showed that the enemy was far from exhausted. If there was light at the end of the tunnel in Indochina, it was elusive, and the American public, increasingly restive, demanded a total review of the principles and assumptions on which American policy had rested since World War II. Critics of containment, the domino theory, and deterrence by military power called into question the wisdom, morality, and expense of the prevailing policies of the United States in Asia.[1] The schisms in the American public went far deeper than partisan politics. Both Hubert Humphrey and Richard Nixon treated the Vietnam issue with caution in the 1968 presidential campaign and failed to stem the tide of protest. Many Americans believed that the mounting casualties and enormous costs of the war were at the root of political dissension, spiritual disillusionment, moral degradation, and economic disaster at home. The pressures mounted to get out of Vietnam and to bring home the prisoners of war. It was obvious that, whichever party won the election in 1968, the new administration would have to come up with a fresh foreign policy, especially in East and Southeast Asia,[2] and the first principle for a new foreign policy must be "no more Vietnams."

In the ensuing reexamination of American interests and policies in Asia, the Philippines was a minor factor. When Americans got around to thinking about the Philippines, they were still inclined to take it for granted that the Philippines would be friendly and supportive of American objectives because of the close, long-standing relationship between the two countries. Their prime concern was that in no case should the

---

[1] U.S. Congress, Senate, Committee on Foreign Relations, *Background Information Relating to Southeast Asia and Vietnam* (7th revised edition), 93rd Congress, 2nd session, December 1974 for chronology of events from 1948 through 1973. Text of President Johnson's address of March 31, 1968 is on pp. 328-336.
[2] Theodore White, *The Making of the President 1968* (New York: Atheneum, 1969).

Americans be induced to intervene in the Philippines as they had done in Indochina.

Nixon and the Philippines. When President Nixon assumed office in 1969, he began the graduated withdrawal of American forces from Vietnam and expedited discussions with North Vietnam in Paris in search of peace with honor. He initiated a policy of détente with the People's Republic of China and the Soviet Union and at Guam proclaimed the doctrine that bore his name. The Nixon Doctrine promised that the United States would keep its treaty commitments; would provide a nuclear shield if a nuclear power should threaten the freedom of an ally or nation whose security was vital to the United States; and, in cases involving other types of aggression, would furnish military and economic assistance when asked and as appropriate. But the United States would look to the nation directly threatened to provide the manpower for its own defense.[3] To Americans, this policy meant no more Vietnams, but to the Filipinos it indicated that they had been downgraded in the American scale of priorities and that in time of trouble they could no longer rely on U.S. assistance.

By way of elaboration of the Nixon Doctrine, various spokesmen for the administration explained that the United States would remain strong in the Pacific as an encouragement to its friends and a deterrent to war, but would no longer immerse itself in the internal affairs of others. The United States would support nationalism, economic development, and modernization in accordance with its interests and commitments. It would not turn its back on any nation of the region but would avoid the creation of situations in which there might be such dependency on the United States as to enmesh the United States inevitably in what were essentially Asian conflicts and problems. The United States wished to extend assistance to the greatest extent possible but in an orderly and judicious manner; it wished to participate as one Pacific nation among several in economic development and the maintenance of stability in Asia.[4]

---

[3] Committee on Foreign Relations, *Background Information*, pp. 356-367. See also *New York Times*, July 26, 1969. Department of State, *United States Foreign Policy 1969-1970*, Publication No. 8575, 1971, pp. 36-37, gives the essence of the Nixon Doctrine in East Asia and the Pacific. For a critique of the doctrine, see Earl C. Ravenal, "The Nixon Doctrine and Our Asian Commitments," *Foreign Affairs*, January 1971, pp. 201-217.

[4] See Senator Mike Mansfield, "Perspective on Asia," Report to the Senate Committee on Foreign Relations, 91st Congress, 1st session, September 13, 1969. Mansfield's report was reprinted in Manila by the U.S. Embassy as *Current Comment*, Philippine-American Relations Series, No. 8.

According to the Nixon Doctrine, the United States would support the expanding political, economic, cultural, and security arrangements among the Asian nations and would assist, where appropriate, in efforts that might be undertaken to strengthen them. The entire region of Southeast Asia—with its 250 million people, vast resources, and strategic location—was of great consequence to the United States. The newly formed nations, however, would have to bear the responsibilities of independence. They would have to hold the containment line with their own strength and put down their own insurgents. American intervention could not again be called for except in the unlikely event of overt aggression by outside forces. Underdeveloped nations would have to look to Japan, Australia, New Zealand, Germany, and the rest of Western Europe for help in satisfying their rising expectations. The proliferation of contacts between Socialist and non-Socialist countries in Asia, too, was entirely in accord with the announced American desire for a lower U.S. profile in Asia. It suited the Americans to see Southeast Asia become a zone of peace, freedom, and neutrality.

Repeated assurances were also given by administration spokesmen to the effect that the new directions in American policy would not lead to neoisolationism. The American military presence in Southeast Asia and the Western Pacific would be reduced in an orderly fashion, but the American role in Asia would not shrink from overinvolvement to noninvolvement. The United States would not withdraw precipitously to Fortress America and leave its friends, particularly in the Philippines, helpless before the menace of China, Russia, and possibly Japan.

After his pronouncement on Guam, President Nixon went to Manila to exchange ideas with President Marcos regarding U.S.-Philippine relations. Upon arrival in Manila, President Nixon said, "We are closer to the Philippines than to any other people in Asia . . . we are good friends even if our relations are strained." He declared that the United States wanted a new era—instead of the old special relationship, a new relationship based on mutual trust, respect, confidence, and cooperation. The United States would play its part and provide its fair share, but, Nixon warned, peace in Asia could not come from the United States, it must come from Asia. As he departed, Nixon again promised assistance and cooperation. He referred to the American military presence in the Philippines as a guarantee of the independence the Filipinos had fought so hard to win and promised material support in the fight against subversion. Then, revising the statement he had made upon arrival, Nixon said, "We *have* a special relationship with the Philippines which will always be in our hearts, but we also recognize the force of nationalism which is the wave of the future." [5]

The Effects of Stalemate in Vietnam. During the first Nixon administration the protracted negotiations in Paris and the continuing withdrawal of American troops from Vietnam, coupled with the ineffective escalation of hostilities in Cambodia and Laos, provoked further demonstrations in the United States and deepened doubts in the Philippines about the wisdom and the sincerity of the U.S. presence in Southeast Asia. The evolution of U.S. policy in Asia looked different in the Philippines than it looked in the United States. Speeches by public figures in the United States, the debates in Congress, and articles in the press to the effect that the cold war had ended, that ideologies had lost their punch, that American military predominance had been replaced by a balance of power, that American economic supremacy had disappeared, and that the new spirit of nationalism and independence had reduced the dangers of external aggression had an ominous ring to the Filipinos, who felt that they were about to be jilted or displaced in the affections of the Americans. But throughout the early seventies, the United States gave assurances to friendly nations in Asia, including the Philippines, that it would not move with undue haste and would reduce its contribution to Asian security only as the Asian nations could pick up the slack. The United States would never abandon Asia, President Nixon pledged, but it would not conceive all the plans, design all the programs, execute all the decisions, and undertake all the defense of the free nations of the world.[6]

The joint communiqué issued in Shanghai at the end of President Nixon's visit to China stated that neither side would seek hegemony in the Asia-Pacific region and that each was opposed to efforts by any other country or group of countries to establish such hegemony.[7] This brought little comfort to the Philippines even though détente was an article of faith in Manila as well as in Washington. The Philippine

---

[5] Department of State, *Bulletin,* August 25, 1969, pp. 141-146.

[6] Richard Nixon, *U.S. Foreign Policy for the 1970's,* a report to the Congress, February 18, 1970, p. 7.

[7] Richard Nixon, *U.S. Foreign Policy for the 1970's,* a report to the Congress, May 3, 1973, p. 20. See also Department of State, "Issues in U.S. Foreign Policy," No. 4, The People's Republic of China, Publication No. 8666, 1972. The text of the Shanghai communiqué is on p. 43.

government was concerned about the growing disenchantment in the United States over Asian adventures and the diminishing inclination of Congress and the American public to support foreign aid. The new American skepticism about the efficacy of the military in foreign relations, the devious machinations of the CIA, and the hardening American attitudes toward overseas commitments left Philippine officials uneasy. The investigations of the Symington subcommittee of the Senate Foreign Relations Committee into American commitments in the Philippines, meanwhile, angered President Marcos. All these factors undeniably influenced his decision to proclaim martial law.

The imminent prospect of peace in Vietnam contributed substantially to the reelection of President Nixon in the fall of 1972. The conclusion of the cease-fire agreements of 1973 and the return of American prisoners of war increased his popularity at home, but the revelations of Watergate were quick to undermine it and the persistence of fighting in Indochina made many Americans skeptical about the administration's purposes in Southeast Asia. A majority of the public, as reflected in the Congress, wanted an end to bombing and total disengagement from Indochina. The feeling persisted that the government had not put all its cards on the table for public scrutiny and might take advantage of some legal loophole to return in force to Indochina or to intervene elsewhere in Southeast Asia, specifically Thailand or the Philippines, in the sacred name of resisting aggression.[8]

This skepticism was reflected in repeated attempts by Congress to curb the President's power over military spending and the use of armed forces overseas. The Tonkin Gulf Resolution was repealed and on November 7, 1973, the War Powers Resolution was enacted. This act directed the President in every possible instance to consult with Congress before, and regularly during, the commitment of the armed forces to hostilities or situations where hostilities might be imminent; required that the President make a formal report to Congress whenever, without a declaration of war or other specific congressional authorization, he

---

[8] New York Times, *The Pentagon Papers* (New York: Bantam Books, Inc., 1971) and Daniel Ellsberg, *Papers on the War* (New York: Simon and Schuster, 1972). These books aroused American emotions and increased American uneasiness about Vietnam and all of Southeast Asia and made both houses of Congress more assertive of their rights and responsibilities in matters of foreign policy. The Senate Committee on Foreign Relations, 91st Congress, 2nd session, 1970, printed a pamphlet, "Background Information Relating to Peace and Security in Southeast Asia and Other Areas," which compiled the various bills and resolutions designed to curb the powers of the executive.

took significant action committing the armed forces to hostilities abroad or to the risk thereof or substantially increased combat forces on foreign territory; and denied the President the authority to commit armed forces for more than 120 days without congressional approval, while also allowing Congress to order the President to disengage from combat operations at any time before the expiration of the 120-day period.[9] The act was bad news for any of the governments—Cambodia, Laos, Vietnam, Thailand, or the Philippines—that might have been tempted to rely upon unpublicized agreements with or assurances from the American executive. Any subsequent use of the armed forces would have to conform to the congressional prescription, as was subsequently demonstrated in President Ford's military action in Cambodia following the capture of the American ship *Mayaguez* in the spring of 1975.[10]

Reexamination of SEATO. The same skepticism about prevailing policies in Southeast Asia prompted the Senate to conduct a reexamination of the American interest in the Southeast Asia Treaty Organization (SEATO). The fundamental questions were whether SEATO had outlived its usefulness and whether the Manila Pact still provided a legal basis on which the United States might be obliged to intervene with its armed forces in Thailand or the Philippines.[11]

In signing the Manila Pact in 1954, the United States had recognized that armed aggression against any of the parties (including the Philippines) would endanger its own peace and safety and had promised in that event to act to meet the common danger in accordance with its constitutional processes. If any party to the pact were threatened in any way other than by armed attack (for example, by subversion or insurgency) the parties would consult immediately to agree on measures

<hr />

[9] U.S. Congress, House of Representatives, Subcommittee on International Security and Scientific Affairs of the Committee on International Relations, "The War Powers Resolution: Relevant Documents, Correspondence, Reports," 94th Congress, 1st session, April 23, 1975. This publication contains the text of the War Powers Resolution, which, on its enactment on November 7, 1973, became Public Law 93-148.

[10] Secretary of State Henry Kissinger, "The Mayaguez Rescue," Press Conference, May 16, 1975. Also Senator Mike Mansfield, "The Mayaguez Incident," as discussed on *Face the Nation,* May 18, 1975 and printed in the *Congressional Record,* Senate, p. 8818. A four part document, "Seizure of the Mayaguez," consisting of Hearings and the appropriate Reports of the Comptroller General of the United States, was issued by the House Committee on International Relations, 94th Congress, 1st and 2nd sessions, 1975 and 1976.

[11] U.S. Congress, Senate, Committee on Foreign Relations, *U.S. Commitment to SEATO,* 93rd Congress, 2nd session, March 6, 1974.

to be taken for the common defense. The Manila Pact had been interpreted to mean that Communist-inspired insurgency constituted aggression by armed attack and had been used as the rationale for the Tonkin Gulf Resolution and the Rusk-Thanat agreement that sent U.S. marines into Thailand in 1962. Congress feared that the pact might again be used to justify intervention in Thailand or a military response to a possible distress call from the government of the Philippines.

The Senate hearings on SEATO, published on March 6, 1974, revealed the intensity of anti-SEATO feeling in the United States and the degree to which this centered about the Philippines. SEATO was criticized as a denial of the objective of a lower U.S. profile in Southeast Asia and an obstacle to better understanding with the People's Republic of China. It tended to encourage Thailand and the Philippines to spend money on security that ought to be invested in development and served as a prop for reactionary governments, diluting their efforts to come to terms with their own internal tensions.[12]

The strongest argument against SEATO was its effect on Philippine-American relations. SEATO seemed to offer the Philippines a false hope and seemed to obligate the United States to a military commitment that it was determined to avoid. To some Americans, the sensible course was to do away with SEATO entirely. This was not agreeable to the State Department, however, which pointed out that SEATO had provided a military shield behind which economic life had improved and that the American presence in SEATO had contributed to the growing self-confidence of former European colonies and to the growing sense of security in the Southeast Asia region. It was further argued that SEATO might still provide useful opportunities for military muscle flexing and give some psychological support to Thailand and the Philippines. In the game of power politics in the Pacific, furthermore, SEATO was not unwelcome to the People's Republic of China. China could use SEATO as a counter to Japan and the U.S.S.R., and in return China might be persuaded to limit itself in the Paracels and proceed with caution in the Spratley Islands. If SEATO could be used in any way as a bargaining chip, it would be foolish, said the State Department, to give it

---

[12] Ibid., p. 3. Robert S. Ingersoll, assistant secretary of state for East Asia and Pacific affairs, stated the case for the government. George McT. Kahin of Cornell (p. 35) and Bernhard K. Gordon of the University of New Hampshire (p. 44) presented more skeptical points of view on the value of SEATO. Robert D. Shuey, analyst in Asian affairs, and Larry A. Niksch, analyst in Asian affairs, Congressional Research Service, Library of Congress, prepared for the hearing an informative article, "The Role of SEATO in U.S. Foreign Policy" (p. 63).

up without receiving a concession of equal diplomatic value in return. Finally, the State Department argued, Southeast Asia had already received enough shocks; the demise of SEATO would be unnecessarily cruel. The hearings on SEATO did not lead to legislation, largely because the climactic events in the United States in the summer of 1974 shifted the nation's attention from Southeast Asia to the resignation of President Nixon. For the moment, the question of SEATO was pushed aside.

President Ford and the Philippines

The Filipinos were not particularly aroused by the revelations of Watergate but they were immeasurably impressed by the fact that the constitutional system in the United States was sufficiently strong to bring about the removal of a President. They were also a little perturbed to see Nixon go. Although they had failed to make substantial progress in negotiating with the United States on a single issue during the Nixon administration, they felt that Nixon had been understanding and sympathetic in dealing with the Philippines. With Nixon in the White House, the Filipinos believed they could live with the Nixon Doctrine. With his successor they were not so sure.

On August 14, 1974 President Ford addressed a note to President Marcos promising that he would deal openly with allies and adversaries and maintain a strong defense policy as the surest way to peace in Asia and pledging continuity in the support of the United States for the security, independence, and economic development of the Philippines. He assured President Marcos of the importance that the United States attached to the long-standing relationship between their two countries and affirmed that he was fully committed to honoring all treaties, agreements, and understandings that existed between the United States and the Philippines. Ford ended his note by saying, "In these important endeavors, I will have the support of Secretary Kissinger, in whom I have the greatest confidence." [13]

In the effort to fit the Philippine segment into the new jigsaw puzzle of defense in the Pacific, in September 1974 the State Department issued a new formulation of the Nixon Doctrine specifically applying to the Philippines, which it pointedly described as "an important ally of the United States in Asia." This stated:

[13] The White House, "Correspondence between President Ford and President Marcos," Press Release, August 9, 1974, the day that President Ford assumed office.

(1) the United States will honor its commitments by providing a shield for the freedom of an ally; (2) conventional defense is the responsibility of the country directly concerned, with the United States assisting where it will make a difference and where U.S. interests are involved; (3) insurgencies are best handled by threatened governments with police, paramilitary action, and economic and social reforms; and (4) new commitments by the United States will be viewed in the light of careful assessment of U.S. national interests, specific threats to those interests, and U.S. capacity to contain those risks at an acceptable risk and cost.[14]

This was much more cautious and restrained than the original doctrine enunciated by President Nixon five years earlier. It reflected the growing concern of Americans over the gap between commitments and current capabilities and the need to define precisely the nature and extent of commitments, expressed or implied.

When President Ford traveled to Vladivostok for his summit meeting with Secretary Brezhnev in the fall of 1974, he visited Japan and Korea but not Manila. At no time did he make any pronouncement of policy that could be interpreted as sanctioning martial law in the Philippines. Instead he took the position that the nature of the Philippine government was a domestic problem over which the United States had no jurisdiction. In his state of the world address on April 10, 1975, the President said the United States would stand by its friends and honor its commitments, but the Philippines was not among the countries enumerated as friends. The omission was noted in Manila.[15]

The Stamp of the Ford Administration. The catastrophic collapse of South Vietnam and the fall of Saigon at the end of April sent shock waves throughout Asia. These events aroused immediate fears that the United States would scuttle and run, retreating into a new isolationism. For the sake of its own credibility and in order to strengthen the shaky structure of peace, the United States found it necessary to make a strong, dramatic reaffirmation of its continuing commitment to policies that had been badly bruised in the Vietnam experience. Modifications, of course, would have to be made to suit the new circumstances.

---

[14] Department of State, "Background Notes: The Philippines," September 1974, p. 8.

[15] This address, delivered in the shadow of impending doom in Indochina, was subject to closest scrutiny throughout Asia. The President mentioned Japan, the Republic of Korea, China, Australia, New Zealand, Singapore, and Indonesia, but not a word about the Philippines. No wonder the Filipinos were disturbed.

The occasion for the redefinition of U.S. policy in Asia was the meeting of the Japan Society in New York on June 18, 1975. The speaker, Secretary of State Kissinger, promised that the United States would not concentrate on Europe to the detriment of Asia. The primary principles of American foreign policy in Asia, he said, were: peace depends upon a stable global equilibrium; without security there can be no effective foreign policy; peace ultimately depends upon reconciliation among nations; without strength and security there can be no conciliation; and peace depends upon a structure of economic cooperation that reflects the aspirations of all peoples.[16]

In laying down guidelines for the conduct of policy in each sub-region of Asia, the secretary said the chief focus of American concern, the only vital interest of the United States in Asia, was Japan—a permanent friend and partner in building a world of progress, the anchor of peace in Northeast Asia, and the counterpoise for the might of the Soviet Union and China. He did little to enhance the credibility of the United States in the Philippines when he added that since the good health of the alliance with Japan was the cornerstone of the administration's Asian policies, the United States had a fundamental interest in preserving the good will and support of Japan in dealing either with China or Southeast Asia.

The Ford administration gave less priority to China than to Japan but more to China than to the Philippines. Following on the Shanghai communiqué, it was in no hurry to normalize relations with China, particularly since Peking seemed willing to accept the residual American military presence in Southeast Asia. Ford was not ready to move as fast as Marcos in cutting ties with Taiwan and courting the People's Republic of China. Because the Chinese urge to expand, if it existed, was checked by the split in the Sino-Soviet bloc, the rise of Japan, the weakness of China itself, and the strength of indigenous nationalism in the new nations of Southeast Asia, the United States did not anticipate the development of any situation in Southeast Asia that might call for military intervention against China.[17]

---

[16] Department of State, Press Release, June 18, 1975.

[17] For unofficial analyses of U.S. interests and policies, see Ralph N. Clough, *East Asia and U.S. Security* (Washington, D.C.: Brookings Institution, 1975), especially Chapter 2, "Reassessing U.S. Interests," pp. 28-44, and William P. Bundy, "New Times in Southeast Asia," *Foreign Affairs,* January 1971, pp. 187-201. Both of these perceptive studies contribute to a better understanding of the environment in which President Ford announced his Pacific doctrine.

Within the general framework of these guidelines, U.S. interests everywhere in Southeast Asia, including the Philippines, were judged to be of great importance but not vital or worth fighting for. The subregion of Southeast Asia was no longer considered militarily crucial since no major power could get at another by way of Southeast Asia and no great power need fear another's pressure there. In the view of the United States, peace in Southeast Asia would be achieved only by preserving the independence of individual nations, satisfying the aspirations of the 250 million inhabitants of the region, improving their rate of economic progress, providing for regional cooperation, and maintaining an equilibrium of power where no outside nation (including the United States) or group of nations could achieve hegemony by external attack or support for internal subversion.

The United States was concerned with the preservation of freedom and civil rights in the region but not to the extent of fighting to preserve a democratic government. Free access to the resources of Southeast Asia, too, was essentially secondary. The United States could find substitutes for everything it bought there and could survive economically in spite of the possible loss of its Southeast Asian markets and investments.

The loss of Indochina and the forced withdrawal of U.S. armed forces from Thailand damaged the prestige of the United States but constituted no threat to its existence. Washington felt no great sense of loss subsequently when the Council of Ministers of SEATO on September 23, 1975, decided to abolish the organization, which had become in their view obsolete and unnecessary.[18] In spite of the progressive reduction of the American military presence in Asia, the influence of the United States in the ideological, diplomatic, economic, and cultural fields remained strong. A significant defense capability continued in the Philippines, Japan, Korea, Taiwan, and the Seventh Fleet remained based in the Pacific. Enjoying good relations with Indonesia, Singapore, Malaysia, and Burma and expressing unmitigated approval of ASEAN as a force for self-reliance, stability, and progress, President Ford deemed it useful to restate the American commitment to Asia in terms that would merit the continued confidence of friends and allies in the purposes and intentions of the United States.

---

[18] *Far Eastern Economic Review,* October 10, 1975, p. 18. Although SEATO was abolished, it was not clear whether the fundamental Southeast Asia Collective Defense Treaty was also terminated.

Ford's New Pacific Doctrine. On December 7, 1975, President Ford, returning from a trip to China, Indonesia, and the Philippines, performed a scissors job on American policy statements made in the six years since the proclamation of the Nixon Doctrine and put the pieces together in a speech delivered in Honolulu.[19] The only difference between what Ford called his New Pacific Doctrine and the former Nixon Doctrine was a matter of circumstance: the former was attuned to a time of peace, the latter to a time of war. President Nixon had sought to achieve peace with honor, President Ford to make the most of it.

Once again President Ford professed his dedication to America's nonpartisan policy of pursuing peace through strength and seeking peace with all and hostility toward none. To assure his nervous Pacific-Asian allies of his conviction that world stability and American security depended upon commitments to Asia, he declared at the outset, "America, a nation of the Pacific Basin, has a vital stake in Asia and a responsibility to take a leading part in lessening tensions, preventing hostilities and preserving peace."

Ford laid down six premises for his New Pacific Doctrine. The first four of these were: (1) American strength is basic to any stable balance of power in the Pacific, essential for American security and for the preservation of the sovereignty and independence of American friends and allies; (2) partnership with Japan is a pillar of our strategy; (3) relations with the People's Republic of China must be normalized and the principles of coexistence and opposition to any form of hegemony in Asia or in any other part of the world accepted by both parties; and (4) the United States continues to have a stake in the stability and security of Southeast Asia. He called the Republic of the Philippines "one of our oldest allies," and said, "Our friendship demonstrates America's long-standing interest in Asia."

The fifth tenet of Ford's Pacific doctrine was (5) the belief that peace in Asia depends upon the resolution of outstanding political conflicts. Ford referred particularly to Korea and Indochina, saying that time would have a healing effect and American policies toward the new regimes on the Indochina peninsula would be determined by their conduct toward the United States. "We are prepared to reciprocate gestures of good will," he said. "If they exhibit restraint toward their neighbors and constructive approaches to international problems, we will look to

---

[19] Department of State, "President Ford's Pacific Doctrine," News Release, Honolulu, Hawaii, December 7, 1975.

the future rather than to the past." Perhaps an old adversary like Hanoi could become a new friend like Japan.

The sixth point in the New Pacific Doctrine was (6) that peace in Asia required a structure of economic cooperation reflecting the aspirations of all the peoples in the region. As a result of the growth of the Asia-Pacific economy, the United States would no longer stand in relation to its allies as donor to dependent but would deal with them as partners in the transfer of scientific and technical knowledge. The President pointed out that U.S. trade in the Pacific Basin now exceeded U.S. trade with Europe.

In conclusion the President noted that the one common theme expressed by the leaders of every Asian country he had visited (presumably including China) was that the United States should continue to exercise steady and responsible leadership. The United States, as the world's strongest nation, had the obligation to use its power to preserve the sovereignty of its Asian allies, to deter aggression, and to contribute to a new structure of stability founded on a balance among the major powers. Secretary Kissinger elaborated upon this statement of general principles, without essentially modifying it, during the last days of the Ford administration.

These statements on the part of the American executive were intended to reaffirm the commitment of the United States to its oft-stated principles of policy. They were recognized as so doing in the Philippines, although they were interpreted not only as a moral commitment to principles but also as a moral commitment to the security and welfare of the Philippine Republic, an American ally. It was acknowledged that these statements were not legally binding and would lead to no positive action except as the Americans might undertake in their own self-interest.

The Nixon Doctrine and Ford's New Pacific Doctrine lapsed with the inauguration of President Carter and placed only such obligations on the new administration as it chose to accept. President Carter was free to reaffirm or deny all or any part of past policy that he deemed no longer in the national interest. Nevertheless, those doctrines were on the record—along with the earlier promises of John Foster Dulles, Dwight Eisenhower, John Kennedy, and Lyndon Johnson—and they exerted an undeniable influence on the policy makers who were obliged to conduct negotiations on the continuing specific issues of U.S.-Philippine relations.

Mutual Security Problems

The principal issues between the United States and the Philippines derive from conflicts of interest in the definition of commitments, revision of agreements on the bases, the maintenance of force levels, the continuance of military assistance, and possible American involvement in the Philippine problems of insurgency and incipient rebellion. Cognizant of the strategic value of the Philippines and appreciative of the importance of maintaining Philippine confidence and good will, the United States seeks to discover and implement the best policies for meeting the security requirements of both nations without risking another war in Southeast Asia.

The Mutual Defense Treaty. The basic commitment to the Philippines, as noted above, is contained in the Mutual Defense Treaty of 1951 which was concluded in the interval between the truce and the armistice in the Korean War. It was seen as a benefit by both sides. For the Philippines it was a safeguard against the resurgence of Japan and a guarantee of American support in the event that the Huk insurgency should get out of hand. For the Americans it was a small price to pay for the Philippine signature on the conciliatory peace with Japan and for the winning of an ally against what appeared at the time to be an aggressive Communist monolith. According to the treaty, each party recognized that an armed attack in the Pacific area on either of the parties would be dangerous to its peace and safety and declared that it would act to meet the common danger in accordance with its constitutional processes. An armed attack under the treaty included an armed attack on the metropolitan territory of either of the parties or on the island territories under its jurisdiction in the Pacific or on its armed forces, public vessels, or aircraft in the Pacific.

The Philippines was gratified by the fact that the treaty was accompanied by stepped-up military and economic assistance.[20] However, it

---

[20] The exact figure for amounts of military and economic assistance given to the Philippines is difficult to determine. The Department of Defense, *Congressional Presentation Book, FY 1975* (p. 138) gives the figure $1,123 million for military assistance given up to that time and includes many items turned over to the Philippines at the close of World War II. The U.S. Agency for International Development, "U.S. Overseas Loans and Grants and Assistance from International Organizations," May 1974, gives the amounts of military grants to the Philippines from 1946 to 1973 as $709.7 million (p. 77). It is often difficult to determine what is listed as military assistance and what as economic aid for security assistance. Terminology is often ambiguous and methods of cost accounting are far from consistent within the separate agencies of the government.

failed to meet Philippine demands for an automatic American response to any attack on the Philippines and lacked any commitment to fight until victory or even to go to war. Furthermore, under its definition of armed attack, the treaty could conceivably commit the Philippines to taking action on behalf of the United States which would be more in the interest of the United States than that of the Philippines. The United States was pleased with the treaty because it pledged the United States only to a line of action that it would have taken even without a treaty since the Philippines had always been inside the defense perimeter of the United States in the Western Pacific. No stronger commitment could have been made lest the Senate, then reeling under the impact of Senator McCarthy and chary of any sort of alliance, refuse to ratify it. On the basis of the limited formula of taking action in accordance with its constitutional processes, the United States persuaded the Philippines to follow in the footsteps of Australia and New Zealand and join with the United States in forging a chain of defense against the Communist powers in Asia. By serving notice to the world that the United States and the Philippines were bound together by common interests, the treaty certainly contributed to stability in Southeast Asia and perhaps to the deterrence of aggression.

In the midst of general concern about the possibility of expanded Communist activities in Southeast Asia after Dien Bien Phu in 1954, the Philippines was prompted to raise questions about the action it could expect from the United States should hostilities spread. In a note to the foreign secretary of the Philippines, Secretary Dulles said:

> Under our Mutual Defense Treaty and related actions, there have resulted air and naval dispositions of the United States in the Philippines, such that an armed attack on the Philippines could not but be also an attack upon the military forces of the United States. As between our nations, it is no legal fiction to say that an attack on one is an attack on both. It is a reality that an attack on the Philippines is an attack on the United States.[21]

This affirmation, given without benefit of congressional assent, went beyond the words of the original treaty and seemed to satisfy the Philippines during the next few years. This was the phase when SEATO was coming into existence and the Khrushchev-Chou En-lai formulation of

---

[21] *Symington Hearings*, p. 6. The quote of Secretary Dulles is included in the testimony of James M. Wilson, Jr., Deputy Chief of Mission, Manila, who was giving for the Senate subcommittee a history of the U.S. association with the Philippines.

peaceful coexistence seemed to have removed the immediate danger of war. It was accepted in the Philippines as a moral commitment on the part of the United States. The Philippines again became uneasy about the degree of protection afforded them by the Mutual Defense Treaty, however, when the Chinese began to mutter about the East Wind prevailing over the West Wind and shelled the offshore islands. President Garcia visited President Eisenhower in 1958 and at the conclusion of his visit, the two presidents issued a joint communiqué intended to put the Filipinos more at ease. It stated that, in accordance with existing alliances and the deployments and dispositions thereunder, any armed attack against the Philippines would involve an attack against the United States forces stationed there and would be instantly repelled. The next year, U.S. Ambassador Bohlen and Philippine Foreign Secretary Serrano concluded a formal memorandum in which the United States expressly reaffirmed the Dulles note and the Eisenhower-Garcia communiqué, but at no time was there any evidence that Congress would have been willing to incorporate such sweeping statements as these into the formal treaty structure.

The Kennedy administration never issued a statement of policy with respect to the Philippines, but President Johnson undertook to give the Philippines some new assurances. The occasion was the visit of President Macapagal to Washington in 1964, when Johnson was eager to get the Philippines to show the flag in Vietnam. The joint communiqué at the end of that visit repeated verbatim the earlier Eisenhower-Garcia communiqué, thus pledging the Democratic administration to the commitments that had been made by its Republican predecessor. With the heating up of the war in Vietnam and the change of presidents in the Philippines, Johnson felt that he should again put the American commitment on the record. In 1966 at the end of a state visit to Washington, President Marcos was assured by President Johnson that the policy of the United States regarding mutual defense continued to be as stated by him and by past U.S. administrations to the Philippine government since 1954. In September 1968 the U.S. ambassador delivered an *aide-mémoire* to President Marcos which renewed the assurance that the Mutual Defense Treaty remained in full force.[22]

As developments in Vietnam deepened doubts about the American commitment in the Philippines and caused Marcos to undertake new diplomatic initiatives to reduce his reliance on the United States, the

[22] Ibid., p. 7.

115

first forebodings of disaster prompted the United States to undertake a fundamental reexamination of all security agreements and commitments abroad beginning with the Mutual Defense Treaty with the Philippines. It was pertinent to explore whether past commitments were in accord with new statements of doctrine and compatible with the pursuit of détente with the Communist powers. With regard to the Philippines, the overriding concern of some members of Congress was to make it clear that the phrase "armed attack" should be interpreted to mean "external armed attack" and thus to exclude insurgency. Their fear was that the Philippine treaty, originally designed to enhance security, had become a potential threat to American security in that it could drag the United States into an unwanted war. If the proposition were accepted that the Philippines was no longer a vital interest of the United States, not even the costs of successful military intervention would be justified. Therefore the risks of intervention must be minimized. But there was no predisposition to accomplish this by an abrupt termination of the treaty. It was still assumed that the Philippines needed American protection and that it was in the American interest to preserve as strong a strategic toehold as possible in Southeast Asia.

During the investigations conducted before the Symington subcommittee of the Senate Foreign Relations Committee, specific problems bearing on the nature and extent of the treaty commitment to the Philippines were discussed. If the Philippines should provoke an attack, would the United States be obligated to intervene? If the Philippines should precipitate an incident in Sabah producing a reaction from Malaysia, how would this affect the United States? How could an American response in that instance be reconciled with the desire to keep out of intraregional quarrels? If the Philippines were to become involved in the conflict over the sovereignty of the Spratley Islands or the search for offshore oil, would the United States be obligated to take action on behalf of the Philippines? If the Philippines were to take preventive measures to thwart alleged aggression on the part of unified Vietnam or China, would the United States be required to support the Philippine initiative? If an external attack were to be made on one of the Philippine islands where no American forces were stationed, would this make a difference in the American response? [23]

---

[23] Questions such as these were raised primarily by Senator Fulbright. They appear throughout the hearings and were addressed to government witnesses including the deputy chief of mission, Manila, and the commanding officers at Clark Air Base and the Subic Bay Naval Base.

No definitive answers were possible for questions such as these, but the hearings revealed that even under the treaty the United States could expect little help from the Philippines in the event of an armed attack and there were definite limits to what the Philippines could anticipate from the United States. The fact that such questions arose meant to the Philippines that U.S. commitments would be honored, to be sure, but that they would be given the strictest possible construction. Any inferences about the strength of moral commitments would have to be tested against the legal commitments endorsed by the Congress.

No legislative action followed the Symington hearings because of the agonizing preoccupation of achieving peace in Indochina. From 1969 to 1975, the United States endeavored to maintain the confidence of its friends and allies and struggled to regain the prestige lost by its apparent defeat and humiliation in Southeast Asia. During that period, it would have been unwise to tamper with the long-range commitment to the Philippines. But in the rapidly evolving struggle for a new balance of power in Asia and the Pacific region, the diminished value of the Mutual Defense Treaty became more apparent. The treaty was no longer relevant as a guarantee against the rising power of Japan. Born of the cold war, it was not compatible with the new doctrine that the political orientation of the nations of Southeast Asia had ceased to be vital to the United States. Russia seemed to be as interested as the United States in stability in Asia, and China seemed again to be satisfied with peaceful coexistence. With the replacement of the old idea of containment by the new policy of détente, it followed that old alliances based on ideological confrontation should give way to new arrangements seeking multilateral cooperation.

But with the total retreat from Indochina in 1975 and the unfolding of Marcos's New Developmental Diplomacy under martial law, the wisdom of postponing any positive action on the treaty became readily apparent. It was not realistic to assume that modifications could be accomplished which would satisfy both sides and which at the same time could win the approval of the U.S. Senate. Since there was no overwhelming demand to terminate the treaty, the obvious course was to let it ride. It added nothing to the costs of American security and caused neither the Philippines nor the United States any undue embarrassment. As a defensive alliance, it may have lost some significance but it could conceivably become more important if Russia and China were to join forces in some new concerted Communist drive.

On the other hand, the termination of the Mutual Defense Treaty was not believed to be damaging to American interests. It was important to keep the good will of the Philippines and to accede to its desires if it wanted termination. Even without a treaty the United States remained free to take action according to its constitutional processes in the event of an attack on the Philippines by a nuclear power, and the abolition of the treaty might enlarge the range of options available to the United States in its pursuit of détente. The challenge to the United States in the Philippines was not so much to deter aggression as to come to terms with the dynamics of social change and economic development, and for the achievement of those objectives the Mutual Defense Treaty was not essential.

The treaty issue was mentioned in public announcements but it was not the subject of active negotiations as, for example, the issue of the military bases was. Believing that it was of extreme importance not to undermine stability in Asia and ultimately world peace, President Ford declared that he would permit no question to arise about the firmness of America's treaty commitments or the firmness of its resolve to stand by its allies in Asia.[24] Ford took the position, however, that if any partner of the United States itself wanted to modify its commitments, the United States would be prepared to accommodate that desire. It had no intention to exert unwelcome pressure on a weaker ally. Secretary Kissinger voiced a stern warning on June 23, 1975, applicable to the Philippines:

> No country should imagine that it is doing a favor by remaining in alliance with us. . . . No ally can pressure us by a threat of termination; we will not accept that its security is more important to us than it is to itself. We assume that our friends regard their ties to us as serving their own national purposes, not as privileges to be granted or withdrawn as a means of pressure. Where this is not the mutual perception, then clearly it is time for change.[25]

---

[24] *New York Times,* May 8, 1975, p. 19. Separate assurances were given to the prime ministers of Australia, New Zealand, and Singapore.

[25] Department of State, Press Release, June 23, 1975, "Secretary Kissinger before the Southern Council on International and Public Affairs and the Atlanta Chamber of Commerce," p. 4.

When President Carter inherited the conflicts surrounding the possible modification or termination of the defense treaty, one element —the question of human rights—became increasingly controversial. Diplomacy and security in the Pacific area were less critical than they had been during Vietnam and Americans in and out of Congress deeply concerned with human rights seriously questioned the wisdom of continuing a treaty commitment which had lost much of its original justification. How could it serve the American national interest to maintain an alliance with a nation that had turned its back on American principles and could sustain itself only by resorting to authoritarian government? [26]

Military Bases and Force Levels. The security issues deriving from conflicts of interest in the military bases and the maintenance of American forces in the Philippines were complex and difficult to settle. New judgments had to be made of the value of the military presence of the United States—including air force units, the fleet, and the system of bases anchored by the installations in the Philippines—in the accomplishment of revised American objectives. As the threat of aggression by armed attack diminished and the United States deliberately sought a lower profile, it was inevitable that the bases in the Philippines would lose much of the importance that had been attached to them since World War II, but it was premature to write them off as anachronistic. They were still considered essential for the implementation of American foreign policy and the preservation of regional stability. The major problems were to determine what costs should be paid for the continued use of the bases and what terms could be agreed upon by the United States and the Philippines for making the bases the most effective instruments for mutual defense in a rapidly changing political and diplomatic environment.

When the United States relinquished sovereignty over the Philippines in 1946, military base areas were excluded. The next year an agreement was entered into which governed the right of the United States to use, operate, control, and have access to twenty-three army,

---

[26] U.S. House of Representatives, *Hearings on Human Rights.* Assistant Secretary Habib, Department of State, presented the official point of view that security considerations must take precedence over the form of government in policy determination.

navy, and air force bases in the Philippines.[27] These bases proved to be of immense value to both the United States and the Philippines. For the United States they were vital for ordinary operations of the air force and the Seventh Fleet and for the conduct of hostilities from Korea to Indochina. They were the essential components in a joint system which enabled the United States to provide for the defense of the Philippines against external attacks and gave the Philippine government the strength to put down the Huk insurgency in the 1950s. From 1947 through 1969 the original bases agreement was the subject of intermittent negotiation and modification which included progressive relinquishment of specific land areas, agreement on prior consultation before using the bases for combat operations or introducing long-range missiles, revision of criminal jurisdiction provisions, revision of the original termination date from 2046 to 1991, and addition of arrangements to cover base labor relations and customs procedures.[28]

As of 1977, the chief U.S. installations remaining in the Philippines were Clark Air Base, the second largest air base in the world, and Subic Bay Naval Base, which was so big that it could dry dock major fleet units and reserve its own hillsides for target practice and its beaches for training in amphibious landings. Operations had ended on Mactan Island, off Cebu, in 1969 and two years later Sangley Point had been given over to the Philippines. Other installations remaining were the San Miguel Communications Station in San Antonio, Zambales, Camp John Hay Air Base in Baguio City, a naval station in Poro Point, La Union, and a communications station in Camp O'Donnel in Capas, Tarlac. The two major bases, at the peak of their activity, had been manned by some 35,000 Americans and had given employment to 50,000 Filipinos. The bases were the largest employer of labor in the Philippines after the government and poured between $150 million and $200 million annually into the Philippine economy. By the end of 1974 some 16,000 American military personnel were still stationed at the bases along with 1,076 Department of Defense civilians and 21,548

---

[27] Department of Foreign Affairs, *Agreements between the Republic of the Philippines and the United States of America concerning Military Bases,* Treaty Series, vol. 1 (Manila: 1948), pp. 140-160.

[28] Center for Strategic and International Studies, *U.S.-Philippines Economic Relations* (Washington, D.C.: Georgetown University, 1971), p. 77 ff. lists the major agreements with detailed provisions. See also *Symington Hearings,* p. 11.

dependents. In 1976 the number of U.S. servicemen in the Philippines fell below 14,000.[29]

The uncertainty of the future made it difficult to foresee how permanent the bases would be, but it was agreed that some kind of base system should be preserved as long as both nations wanted it. On the American side, questions were cautiously raised about the continuing utility of the bases. It was asked whether the bases any longer served the political interests of the United States since they antagonized the Filipinos and neither impressed the world as a symbol of American power nor created good will for the United States. They often conjured up unfavorable images of the outmoded British imperial system of the nineteenth century. On the other hand, they tended to thwart the diplomatic purposes of the United States by causing more irritation than sympathy in Southeast Asia, where they represented exactly the kind of big power hegemony that ASEAN was designed to oppose. As long as American bases existed, it would be more difficult to negotiate with Moscow, and possibly Peking, since the extension of American military power to Southeast Asia did nothing to promote the mutual trust that would have to be created if détente diplomacy were to have any hope of success.

It was also questioned whether the bases were worth the costs and whether they could any longer fulfill the mission with which they were charged. The strategic importance of the bases, originally calculated at a time when naval power was supreme and the key to national survival was the command of the seas, no longer obtained now that air power and missiles had become the vital factors in defense. The bases were not equipped to cope with nuclear attack and they were less practical than surface vessels or submarines for launching missiles.

Most of all, so conspicuous and so extensive were the bases that they invited attack and automatically increased the possibility of U.S. military involvement in any insurgency situation. Before Vietnam, it had seemed natural and appropriate to look to the bases for assistance against Communist rebels, but after Vietnam the most frequently expressed objection to the bases was the unwarranted risk that they might

---

[29] The figures for Clark Field and other air force installations are given in the *Symington Hearings,* p. 55; those for Subic Bay and other naval installations are on p. 91. See U.S. Congress, House of Representatives, Subcommittee on Future Foreign Policy Research and Development of the Committee on International Relations, *Shifting Balance of Power in Asia: Implications for Future U.S. Policy,* 94th Congress, 2nd session, 1976. Admiral John S. McCain, Jr., uses the figure of 14,000 in his testimony, p. 180.

afford an excuse for intervention in the internal affairs of the Philippines. If President Marcos should get into deeper trouble with dissident elements, it was feared that he might either assume a more vigorous anti-American posture to strengthen his position as a nationalistic leader or call upon the Americans on the bases to help him restore order. In either case, the bases might prove to be embarrassments. Furthermore, if the revolutionary forces should attack the bases as part of their campaign against the Philippine government, the United States would be identified as pro-Marcos and would be thrust into the thick of the fighting. And if antigovernment forces should prevail, the American bases and forces would surely suffer the consequences of defeat. The American military presence in the Philippines linked the interests of the United States perilously with the martial law regime of President Marcos.

Such considerations as these did not shake the official American position that since the retreat from Vietnam the bases in the Philippines were more important than ever to the United States. They were essential for the control of vital sea lanes and for the peace and stability of Southeast Asia. Even if no immediate threat to the Philippines were perceived and the bases were not likely to be called upon to defend the islands against an armed attack from the outside, they were indispensable for carrying out the global policies of the United States.

Admiral John S. McCain, Jr., testified that the Philippines, with its strategic location, bore a direct relationship to the very survival of America as a free and independent nation. As a guardian of the eastern approaches to the Straits of Malacca, it was vital to the defense of Japan, Australia, and the Indian Ocean. It was the American toehold in that part of the world, representing "our farthest forward outpost, our last dam, our front line trenches and were we to lose the Philippines, our next fall back would be Guam, then Honolulu, and then the State of California." [30]

The bases gave the United States the flexibility and operational efficiency it needed to respond to any contingency and to maintain military readiness in the Western Pacific, McCain said. The two bases, Clark and Subic, were centrally located, free from restrictive operating limitations, fully established and equipped, ideally suited to American needs, and relatively inexpensive to operate. They performed their

---

[30] Committee on International Relations, *Shifting Balance of Power in Asia*, p. 187.

122

function well, which was to maintain an American deterrence posture, support combat operations if deterrence should fail, help to assure a high state of readiness of U.S. forces, maintain the credibility of American commitments in the area, and buttress and sustain the confidence and determination of our friends and allies. Their technical tasks included servicing the fleet and the air force in their patrolling, intelligence-gathering, and ordinary defense operations in East Asia. According to Admiral McCain, the greatest threat to Philippine security would be the Russians, not the Chinese or the Vietnamese; the danger was not necessarily frontal assault or open conflict, but perhaps the supplying of arms and ammunition to some such antigovernment force as the Communists or the Muslims. Therefore the United States should not contemplate leaving the bases in the Philippines. On the contrary, it should consider one of its prime objectives to be retaining the utilization of the bases and full freedom to operate from them. If pressure were brought to bear against the American bases in Japan, Okinawa, and Taiwan, the only U.S. bases left between Hawaii and the Mediterranean would be those in the Philippines and at Diego Garcia in the Indian Ocean, which, McCain said, should be maintained at any cost.

When in 1969 President Marcos asked to enter into negotiations to update the Military Bases Agreement of 1947, as amended, he did not propose to debate the issue whether American bases should be kept or abandoned, he wished only to negotiate mutually agreeable terms for their continued operation. Refusing to be stampeded into precipitate action by extravagant Philippine demands, the American side showed itself disposed to make adjustments that would meet U.S. military requirements, contribute to the defense and economic necessities of the Philippines, and satisfy the *amour-propre* of sensitive Filipinos. Negotiations dragged on through two Republican administrations, only to be passed on to President Carter when he reached the White House. At the outset, Marcos had announced that the problem of sovereignty was not under negotiation—the bases would no longer be American bases in the Philippines, but Philippine bases used by the Americans. He would also insist on removing the last vestiges of extraterritoriality: it would no longer be American law, but Philippine law that would be applied on the bases. The bases would be under the command of a Filipino and the only flag to fly over them would be that of the Philippines. Other matters would be open for discussion, and to these assumptions no serious objections were registered by the Americans.

The first problem for negotiation was how much the Americans should pay for the use of the bases and whether it should be considered rent or military assistance. Should payments be made in kind or in money with the Philippines free to purchase weapons and supplies wherever they could be obtained at cheapest prices? On December 4, 1976, a news story from Washington announced that Secretary Romulo and Secretary Kissinger had agreed on a figure of $1 billion in military and economic aid over the next five years in return for the continued use of the bases.[31] The story was denied by the Filipinos, who suggested that $1 billion might be acceptable for military aid alone, not for military and economic aid combined, and that compensation for use of the bases must be counted as rent, not aid. Marcos said the mentioned figure was too small as compared with the $1.2 billion five-year lease agreement between the United States and Spain and the $1 billion four-year agreement between the United States and Turkey. The proposed term of five years indicated that the terminal date of 1991 currently in effect would be substantially shortened.

Other points of difference complicated the negotiations. The Philippines was no longer content with the formula of Philippine jurisdiction over offenses committed by American service personnel when off base and off duty, but insisted on jurisdiction over all offenses except those committed in the performance of military duty. This went beyond the NATO model jurisdiction agreement of 1965 and resulted from the extreme sensitivity of the Filipinos over the issue of extraterritoriality. Filipinos felt the Americans had taken advantage of their privileged position to thwart the application of Philippine laws in cases occurring in seedy neighborhoods surrounding the bases and involving violent crimes, gambling, prostitution, and dealings on the black market. Americans, on the other hand, felt that in some instances servicemen had been detained too long without trial by the Philippine authorities or subjected to prejudicial procedures. They were not willing to submit quietly to Marcos's general order that servicemen and dependents on base should be under the jurisdiction of the Philippines for such offenses as subversion, sedition, or rebellion. Under martial law, owning a book critical of the Marcos regime could be condemned as subversive.[32]

---

[31] Rodney Tasker, "Back to the Base Issue," *Far Eastern Economic Review,* December 17, 1976, p. 13.
[32] Harvey Stockwin, "The Hurdles that Remain, Issues to be Settled," *Far Eastern Economic Review,* December 17, 1976, p. 14.

Clarification was needed in defining the rights and duties of the base commander because Americans would not accept a situation where a Philippine commander would be placed in charge of American military operations. As American bases, the bases were to be used for the defense of the Philippines against armed attack but also for support of American forces involved in military conflicts with other countries in the area. If and when they became Philippine bases, their function would have to be redefined. As Philippine bases they would no longer be reserved for exclusive American use but would become the heart of the Philippine defense system. They would be at the disposal of the Philippine government for housing, use of equipment, counterinsurgency, or any other military purpose unless otherwise provided. Marcos stated that he would not allow foreign troops to fight on Philippine soil for the defense of the Philippines, which accorded with the American determination not to let the bases become involved in internal conflicts. It was disturbing to the Americans, however, when Marcos issued joint communiqués with the new unified state of Vietnam and other ASEAN members prohibiting the use of bases for direct and indirect aggression and intervention against other countries in the region. Such a precaution seemed uncalled for.

Marcos also asked for further relinquishment of land that he could advantageously use to further his program of land reform or commercial or industrial development. With an eye to using some of the U.S. base land, he concluded a contract with the Japanese Kawasaki firm for the construction of a shipyard on the west coast of the Philippines. He also probed the possibility of opening the bases, once they were under Philippine control, for use by third parties or by all nations following the example of Singapore. As international bases they might be more lucrative earners of foreign exchange than they were as American bases.

Recognizing the economic importance of the bases to the Philippines and the high value placed by the Philippine armed forces on the American connection, the Americans were disposed to drive a hard bargain. They realized, however, that the nationalists in the Philippines disliked the idea that theirs was the only remaining country in Southeast Asia with alien bases on its soil; sooner or later the forces of nationalism would become sufficiently strong to demand the end of the bases system. The Americans were not inclined to view the relinquishment of the bases and the withdrawal of American forces as an unmitigated disaster since this would remove the most probable source of provocation for American intervention. If the prospects for peace and stability were to grow brighter in East Asia, the United States might welcome a further reduction in the military aspects of the American presence which might enhance its ability to contribute to the social transformation and economic development of friendly nations.

In search of the best future U.S. policy, a prestigious study group at the Brookings Institution suggested that it might be wise for the United States to make a categorical declaration of intent to withdraw from the Philippine bases at some specified time. Such a step would favorably affect the prospects of ASEAN neutralization, détente with China, and big-power understanding. In addition, the less committed the United States felt to maintaining military bases, the easier it would be to adjust American policies to unpredictable change in the balance of domestic forces in the Philippines. The whole matter of the bases was under study and inconclusive negotiation when President Carter succeeded Ford in the White House.

The Military Assistance Program. The related U.S.-Philippine security problems inherent in the military assistance program were likewise under continuous review in the early 1970s. The reassessment reached a critical point with the succession of the Carter administration. With the role of the Philippine bases in U.S. policy and operations in East Asia and the Pacific uncertain and with martial law and the pursuit of self-reliance in diplomacy and defense still dominating the policies of the Philippines, the United States was obliged in its own interests to reassess the premises on which the program of military assistance had been conceived and carried out.

U.S. military assistance to the Philippines is as old as the Philippine Republic. In the aftermath of World War II, the prostrate nation was obliged to look to the United States for all its help. With the appropriate authorization from Congress, the United States concluded a military assistance pact with the Philippines which became effective March 21, 1947. The United States agreed to provide a Joint Military Advisory Group (JUSMAG) and military assistance in the training of troops and to turn over to the Philippine government enormous stores of weapons and equipment that were available in the Philippines after the Japanese surrender. The Philippines agreed to purchase the bulk of its military equipment in the United States and to secure U.S. approval of purchases made elsewhere.[33]

Although the Military Bases Agreement and the Military Assistance Agreement were separate, they were popularly regarded as complementary parts of a single arrangement: the bases agreement would guarantee security against armed attack from the outside and the assistance agreement would make the Philippines sufficiently strong to cope with internal subversion. In the early postwar period the agreements together constituted the security component of what was conceived to be a total American commitment to the military strength, political stability, and economic prosperity of the Philippines. In the Philippines, the military assistance pact was looked upon as rent to which it was entitled as compensation for the American bases. When assistance involved American participation against local insurgents, the Filipinos registered no objections to infringements on their sovereignty and asked for more rather than less U.S. involvement. On its part, the United States did not worry about the possibility of all-out intervention and did not shy away from the charge of undue interference in Philippine internal affairs. In the atmosphere of the cold war, both the United States and the Philippines considered Communist-inspired insurgency a threat to mutual security.

Year after year the United States provided arms and equipment, uniforms and supplies, training in the field and in the United States, and practically everything that was needed to make the armed forces of the Philippines effective. The United States also contributed substantial help to the Philippines in its dispatch of a combat infantry battalion to join the United Nations troops fighting in Korea.[34] The advice and support of the American military accounted in large measure for the military and even the political achievements of President Magsaysay. In its first decade, JUSMAG administered $169.3 million to support a wide range of purposes including the training of jet pilots, delivery of training jets, improvement of airfields, training of the forces of the army and navy, and construction of all sorts of military installations. American expenditures were justified on the grounds that they helped maintain the U.S.-Philippine defense partnership in Southeast Asia, assisted the Philippines's efforts to build up its internal defenses,

---

[33] George Taylor, *The Philippines and the U.S.*, p. 129 ff. See also the statement of General Robert H. Warren, deputy assistant secretary of defense for military assistance and sales, *Symington Hearings*, pp. 242-252.
[34] *Symington Hearings*, p. 36.

accelerated economic development through training in the operation and maintenance of equipment that had both military and civilian uses, promoted the regional alliance system, and contributed to the Philippine program for self-reliance.[35] U.S. assistance was a major factor in every effort to expand and modernize the armed forces of the Philippines. The United States had provided practically all the supplies and equipment needed to improve the fire power, mobility, and communications of the Philippine military, and, in addition, it brought more than 11,000 Philippine officers and men to the United States for advanced training in all types of skills. After their return to the Philippines and their retirement from active duty, they constituted a pool of managerial talent for government and industry, the strategic reserve for the technocrats who have kept the Marcos administration moving in high gear since martial law.

The desire for Philippine cooperation in Vietnam prompted the United States to supplement its ordinary military assistance program. As soon as the Philippines agreed to dispatch the Civil Action Group to Vietnam in 1966, the United States granted compensation in the form of logistical support, all necessary equipment, overseas bonuses, and the costs of a replacement unit for duty inside the Philippines. In addition, the United States agreed to provide the Philippines with two extra antismuggling patrol craft, more rifles and machine guns, and equipment for as many as ten engineering construction battalions to build roads and schools and undertake irrigation projects. This boost to public works helped Marcos immensely in his campaign for reelection in 1969.

While fighting continued in Vietnam, the United States brought its own installations in the Philippines to the peak of operating efficiency and contributed generously to the shoring up of Marcos's antismuggling and antisubversion capability. Funds were made available for military construction, and all manner of arms and equipment were turned over to the Philippine armed forces—small aircraft, helicopters, gunships, bombs, and spare parts for the air force; fast patrol craft for the navy; and machine guns, rifles, grenade launchers, ammunition, helmets, and bulletproof vests for the army. Various American military commands in the Philippines conducted training exercises in such activities as amphibious landings, air defense, antiguerrilla operations, and civic action. American officers never participated in actual combat, but they performed useful staff and liaison functions. During the period of U.S.

---

[35] George Taylor, *The Philippines and the U.S.*, p. 149.

involvement in Vietnam the objective of military assistance was to make the Philippine government as strong as possible and to make sure that nothing would happen in the Philippines to interfere with the conduct of the war in Indochina. There was still no fear of intervention in the Philippines or of U.S. over-involvement in Philippine internal affairs.

After the withdrawal of the Philippines from Vietnam and the break between the United States and the Philippines in defense and diplomatic policy, the United States undertook a reexamination of the military assistance program along with that of the treaty commitment and the bases system. The problem was how to adapt the military assistance program to conform to the specifications of the Nixon Doctrine. At the Symington hearings, it was suggested that the United States had been doing too much and the Philippines too little for mutual defense. The United States had gone beyond its original responsibility of defending its ally against external threat and had gone too far in assisting the Philippine government to put down subversion. By 1969 the view was accepted that the external threat, assumed to be Communist China with possible assistance from internal dissident groups, had been overrated.[36] No significant evidence of the involvement of either Soviet or Chinese Communist agents with the various dissident groups was available. The dissident factions in the field and in the cities seemed to operate essentially on an independent national basis.[37]

It was also suggested that the United States should no longer actively help the Philippine government handle the problems of insurgency. It should do no more than establish the matrix for defense, within which the Philippines would have to bear the responsibility for law and order. In view of the growing spirit of nationalism and anti-foreignism in the Philippines and in the light of Marcos's New Developmental Diplomacy, too much American activity was no longer welcome. The Americans themselves were ready to disbar themselves from further participation with the Filipinos in counterinsurgency because of their new conviction that anything that might lead to intervention should be avoided.

---

[36] See testimony of Rear Admiral Draper L. Kauffman, U.S. Navy, commander in chief, Pacific, representative, Philippines; and commander, U.S. naval forces, Philippines, in *Symington Hearings,* beginning p. 44.

[37] See statement of Minister James M. Wilson, Jr., deputy chief of mission, U.S. Embassy, Manila, in *Symington Hearings,* p. 354.

The problems of military assistance were exacerbated with the imposition of martial law. It was one thing to extend military assistance to a government that was dedicated to democratic institutions, but it was quite another to provide military support for an authoritarian government. Criticisms of the military assistance program reflected that uncertainty. It was argued that the United States had been meeting some of the operating expenses of the Philippine defense establishment and picking up the tabs for commercial items that should not have been entered into the assistance budget. Materials from excess stocks in the Philippines or left over from Vietnam had been given away to the Philippines or sold for almost nothing. All sorts of financial chicanery had been resorted to in order to maximize the assistance grants. The General Accounting Office minced no words in charging that the Philippines had frequently let down its end of a bargain, failing to make funds available for the utilization of materials received from the United States or refusing to provide financial support promised for ordinary administrative purposes.[38]

The United States felt that adjustments in the military assistance program would be required to keep the United States from being too closely identified with the Marcos regime. It looked as if U.S. fire power had put Marcos in office and further assistance would keep him there. The more conspicuous the military connection between Marcos and the United States, the more valid would be the charge that he ruled with America's blessing. The wise course seemed to be to stay as far as possible from interference in Philippine domestic affairs. Although it was obvious that American military equipment was being used to counter Muslim insurgency and the Communist guerrillas in the north and central Philippines, it became the policy of the United States to refrain from direct action by its military personnel. Americans were kept out of the Muslim areas, assistance programs were monitored more carefully, and JUSMAG was instructed not to become involved in combat of any kind. Training exercises were no longer permitted in areas where

---

[38] U.S. Congress, House of Representatives, Subcommittee on Asian and Pacific Affairs of the Committee on Foreign Affairs, *Political Prisoners in South Vietnam and the Philippines,* 93rd Congress, 2nd session, 1974, p. 121. This is a report to the Congress by the comptroller general of the United States on military assistance and commitments in the Philippines involving the Departments of State and Defense.

130

hostilities were going on and civic action training was limited to such nonmilitary pursuits as helping build schools, handing out birth control devices, making well water safe to drink, putting up suspension bridges, and inoculating dogs against rabies.[39]

U.S. military assistance to the Philippines amounted to $22.5 million in 1973, $41.1 in 1974, and $32.1 in 1975, a large part of which was earmarked for the construction of a factory on Bataan to manufacture M-16s. As law and order improved in the Philippines and as the economy turned upward, it seemed that the Philippines could afford to pay in cash for the military assistance it was receiving, especially at a time when economic stringencies at home were forcing Americans to be prudent in their overseas expenditures. Furthermore the human rights issue was being pressed more seriously in the United States. In congressional hearings, the assistant secretary of state for East Asian and Pacific affairs, Philip Habib, presented the official point of view: the security relationship, including the military assistance program, was of overriding importance to the United States. He said:

> While we support the Philippine Government's avowed intention to promote improvement in the social, economic and administrative areas, and think that there has been measurable progress in some of these, we do not believe that the ends justify or require the curtailment of human rights. . . . However, we feel strongly that the future of the Philippines and that of its form of government are for the Philippine people to determine, not us.[40]

Habib expressed the concern of the U.S. government regarding the question of human rights and fundamental freedoms, but also the government's conclusion that those concerns should not jeopardize the security relationship. The State Department's position outlined by Habib did not satisfy some witnesses who argued that all military assistance should be cut off until basic civil liberties were restored. They advocated an embargo on the sale and shipment of arms to the Philippines and urged that no rent should be paid for the bases since rent money would only be used for the purchase of arms and ammunition that would in turn be used for harsher and longer repression. These witnesses felt that repression and rebellion fed on each other and that the United States should have no part whatever in perpetuating the

---

[39] *New York Times,* December 31, 1973.
[40] House of Representatives, *Hearings on Human Rights,* p. 312.

vicious circle. The security relationship should be subordinated to the concern for human rights.[41]

When the Foreign Assistance Act of 1974 was passed, it included the Fraser amendment stating that it was the sense of the Congress that, except in extraordinary circumstances, the President should reduce or terminate security assistance to any government that engaged in a consistent pattern of gross violations of human rights or other flagrant denials of the right to life, liberty, and security of the person.[42] Many congressmen served notice that it would be difficult for them to support foreign aid legislation, especially military aid, except in cases where American foreign policy reflected the traditional commitment of the American people to human rights. This was a clear indication to the executive branch of the government and to the Philippines that the military assistance program was in for trouble.

In the Ford administration's last presentation of its international security assistance program, Secretary Kissinger argued the case for continuing military assistance in spite of energy costs, inflation, and an unfavorable balance of international payments.[43] After reminding the Congress of the long-range policy goals of the United States, he stated flatly that security assistance had been one of the cornerstones of U.S. security and world peace throughout the post-World War II years, and still served the general purposes of the United States. When the administration's program was presented to the Congress, it asked for $19.6 million in military assistance for FY 1977 plus $750,000 for training funds and $17.4 million in foreign military sales credits.[44] The material assis-

[41] Ibid. See particularly the testimony of Rev. Bruno Hicks, p. 112, Raul Manglapus, former foreign secretary and senator of the Philippines, p. 107, Rev. Joseph A. O'Hare, p. 120, and Gerald N. Hill, attorney at law for the Lopez family, p. 289. Father Hicks felt that aid should be terminated (p. 119) but Father O'Hare was less positive (p. 132). In the earlier House of Representatives *Hearings on Political Prisoners* Professor Kerkvliet (p. 77) recommended no further appropriations of military or military-related assistance during the continuance of martial law.

[42] U.S. Congress, House of Representatives, Committee on International Relations, *International Security Assistance Act of 1976,* 94th Congress, 2nd session, 1976. Appendix 11, p. 888, prints the bill "To amend the Foreign Assistance Act of 1961 and the Foreign Military Sales Act" Title I—Military Assistance Grant Programs, Human Rights, Sec. 502 B.

[43] Department of State, "International Security Assistance," Bureau of Public Affairs, November 6, 1975. See also Secretary Kissinger's statement to the House Committee on International Relations, "International Security Assistance Act of 1976," 94th Congress, 2nd session, 1976, p. 1.

[44] U.S. Congress, House, Committee on International Relations, *International Security Assistance Act,* p. 228.

tance grant would help complete the equipping of high priority units and would enhance navy and air force lift capability. The grant aid for training programs would focus on projects that would increase the self-sufficiency of the Philippine armed forces in such areas as logistics and management, while the foreign military sales credits would assist in implementing the five-year modernization and expansion program.

These sums were justified on the grounds that the Philippines still needed security assistance and that the United States retained an important military interest in the Philippines because of its strategic location, its commitment to mutual defense, and the maintenance by the United States of facilities at Subic Bay Naval Base and Clark Air Base. The amounts specified were intended to meet the minimum requirements of the Philippines regardless of the outcome of negotiations over the bases and were considered essential if the defense capabilities of the Philippines were to be kept at a satisfactory level and at a price the Philippines could afford. Any sharp reduction or abrupt cutoff of funds might cause ripples with unfavorable effects not only in the Philippines but throughout the Asia-Pacific area where states, anxious to preserve their independence, were eager to see the United States remain politically engaged because of their feeling that no equilibrium could long be maintained there without U.S. participation.[45] Furthermore, by helping the Philippines develop a more self-reliant defense position, the United States would demonstrate its will and capacity to perpetuate its influence in the Asian balance of power and make manifest its intention to play a constructive role in the area.

The security assistance program passed in the Congress without serious reduction for the Philippines in spite of attempts to cut allotments to the Philippines by two-thirds. The advocates of human rights succeeded in tightening the Fraser amendment with the provision that no military assistance might be given to any government that engaged in a consistent pattern of gross violations of internationally recognized human rights. This was the same provision that had been included in the Foreign Assistance (nonmilitary) Act, but a loophole was left in the security assistance legislation by a section permitting the President to make any exceptions he deemed to be in the national interest. This section further provided that the President, upon the request of the International Relations Committee of the House or the Foreign Relations Committee of the Senate, should transmit to the committee a

---

[45] *New York Times,* October 31, 1975.

report setting forth all the available information about human rights and fundamental freedoms in any country receiving American security assistance.[46]

In accordance with that provision, the chairman of the House Committee on International Relations asked the State Department for a report on human rights violations in the Philippines, an evaluation of the recommendations of the Amnesty International report on the Philippines, an evaluation of the report of the Association of Major Religious Superiors in the Philippines entitled "Political Detainees in the Philippines," an evaluation of the response of the Philippine government to allegations of torture, and a list of the reports by nongovernmental organizations that the department had consulted in preparing its report. In reply the State Department transmitted a document entitled "Human Rights Information," which treated President Marcos gently; a list of "U.S. Government Action in the Human Rights Area," which underscored the efforts made by the United States to promote understanding of and adherence to internationally recognized standards of human rights; and an analysis of "U.S. Interests Justifying a Security Assistance Program," which concluded that the U.S. security assistance program should be continued. In the department's view the elimination of the U.S. security assistance program might lessen the ability of the United States to influence the Philippine government on a range of U.S. interests in the Philippines, including the promotion of human rights; might adversely affect the U.S. security position in the East Asian region and elsewhere; and might decrease confidence in U.S. security commitments to many important nations. This report did not satisfy the proponents of human rights in the Congress or the private organizations interested in promoting human rights overseas. In the Philippines it further antagonized the Marcos administration, which felt that its internal affairs were of no official concern to the American government.[47]

The debate in Congress on security assistance to the Philippines revealed the complexities of the problem facing President Carter and the depth of the emotions it aroused. By congressional fiat, grant aid for the Philippines would come to an end with FY 1977 and all sub-

---

[46] *Philippine News,* San Francisco, March 13-19, 1976, gives a convenient backgrounder on "U.S. Foreign Aid and the Human Rights Provision."

[47] U.S. Congress, House of Representatives, "Human Rights and U.S. Policy: Argentina, Haiti, Indonesia, Iran, Peru, and the Philippines." Reports submitted to the Committee on International Relations by the Department of State, 94th Congress, 2nd session, December 31, 1976, p. 28 ff.

sequent military assistance would have to be provided through foreign military sales credits. Majority sentiment in the Congress still favored military assistance to the Philippines, but it was partially offset by a certain amount of ill will generated by the belief that President Marcos was using the bases negotiations as a means of extracting greater amounts of aid from the United States. Furthermore, a growing number of congressmen, disposed to temper their concern for security with their dedication to civil liberty, were inclined to trim the assistance program until President Marcos should demonstrate his willingness to end martial law and restore democratic institutions.

Problems of Economic Policy

While the problems of mutual security were under review, a similar reexamination of economic relations was pursued. New decisions were called for because of the rapid changes taking place in the American economy, the sharpening conflicts between American economic interests and the increasingly assertive forces of economic nationalism in the Philippines, and the expiration of the Laurel-Langley agreement in 1974.

Largely because of the excessive costs of the Vietnam War, unemployment, rising inflation, and the energy crisis, the United States was obliged to pay closer attention to the spiralling economic costs of its global diplomacy. The dollar had lost its unassailable position in international finance and the customary favorable balance of payments was proving more and more difficult to sustain. The affluence previously identified only with Americans was now shared by others—Arabs and the once devastated Germans and Japanese. Just as American military supremacy had been called into question by Russian power, so American economic primacy had to make room for Germany, Japan, and the Arab bloc. This new situation called for belt-tightening that affected all friendly powers, including the Philippines, and the first area to feel the pinch was foreign assistance.

Foreign Assistance. Since 1946 the United States had dispensed large sums in assistance to the Philippines on the assumption that contributing to economic development would strengthen the Philippine government against Communist insurgency and attract the sympathy and support of the Philippines away from neutralism and the Communist bloc and toward the United States and the free world. Technical and economic

135

assistance, as well as military assistance, was considered useful for mutual security. From 1946 to 1973 the total of economic and military assistance alone was calculated to be $2,292 million,[48] without taking into account the additional expenditures for U.S. military operations in the Philippines, official payment for Philippine goods and services, and disbursements by the Veterans Administration and the Social Security Administration in the Philippines, which together amounted to some $300 million per year.[49] The desire to strengthen an ally had also prompted many of the ordinary commercial operations of the Export Import Bank and the Commodity Credit Corporation as well as some of the loans to the Philippines by American firms and banks.

After the inauguration of the American economic assistance program in 1950, American and Philippine government representatives together worked out an annual schedule of grants-in-aid and low-interest loans, acceptable to the Philippines and paid for by the U.S. Congress, designed to implement the foreign policy objectives of the American donor and at the same time promote the economic development of the Philippines. Under this program, hundreds of American specialists in agriculture, finance, industry, and education gave of their time and talents to the Philippines and hundreds of Filipinos were trained in these fields and exposed to American methods and procedures in private business, public administration, public safety, and public health. American aid contributed substantially to rice development and production, rural electrification, airport construction, and air transportation. It exerted a significant impact on education, notably in agricultural, medical, and technical subjects, and helped to shore up the infrastructure on which national development was based.[50]

These positive results were obtained in spite of recurring difficulties. From the beginning Americans and Filipinos concerned with the administration of assistance, as well as critics of the program in the Congress, the university world, and the media recognized its inherent defects. Largely because of prodding by the executive branch, Congress made its annual appropriations for the Philippines despite its doubts. Con-

---

[48] U.S. Senate, "Foreign Assistance and Related Programs, Appropriation Bill, 1975." Calendar No. 94-39, Report from the Committee on Appropriations, 94th Congress, 2nd session, March 17, 1975, p. 11.

[49] Charles E. Angevine, "U.S. Presence and Policies: Economic and Political Aspects," in *Fifth Annual Seminar for Student Leaders* (Manila: U.S. Embassy, 1973).

[50] Center for Strategic and International Studies, *U.S.-Philippine Economic Relations,* p. 6.

tending that the needs of the Philippines were great and the resources of the United States available for the Philippines were extensive but limited, skeptics insisted that with the best will in the world American aid could have little effect on the basic problems of population growth, land reform, industrialization, social justice, public administration, and standards of public service. Throughout the life of the program, Americans argued with Filipinos over the uses to which aid should be put, the distribution of commodities and control of projects within the Philippines, the utilization of counterpart funds, and the resolution of conflicts between U.S. policy wishes and Philippine development demands. Filipinos accused their American benefactors of selfish motives and wasteful procedures and of using the entire aid program as a self-seeking maneuver to keep Filipinos as "hewers of wood and drawers of water." [51]

In spite of arguments and misunderstandings, the Agency for International Development (AID) mission attached to the U.S. Embassy in Manila earned the confidence of the Philippine government. In the summer of 1972, on the eve of the proclamation of martial law, almost 200 inches of rain fell on the plains of Luzon causing terrible floods. AID came dramatically to the rescue of suffering Filipinos through congressional appropriations of $30 million for emergency relief and $50 million for feeding the victims of the flood and assisting in the repair of homes, public buildings, roads, dikes, and irrigation systems. This was perhaps AID's finest moment in the Philippines.

It was short-lived. When President Marcos ended democratic government and revoked civil liberties, he destroyed the foundation on which U.S.-Philippine cooperation had been built. Doubts were immediately expressed in Congress about the propriety of continuing economic assistance to a country, however friendly, that was ruled by martial law. Some of America's best friends in the Philippines were among the victims of the Marcos dictatorship. Thus, the rationale for foreign assistance as a support for common ideals of liberty and democracy was open to question. With the collapse of the United States in Indochina, the entire AID program was subjected to the same reexamination that applied to every other aspect of foreign policy. As Marcos pursued his independent course in diplomacy, it became increasingly clear that AID would exert little or no political influence in the Philippines and would have to depend for its justification on what it could do to help small farmers and the rural poor.

---

[51] Ibid., p. 61.

Beginning in 1975 appropriations for economic assistance to the Philippines were scrutinized more carefully than ever with an eye to avoiding the appearance of supporting totalitarianism. At a level of approximately $50 million per year, aid was concentrated on rural development, family planning, and public health for the prime benefit of the lowest third of Philippine society. All the elements of the U.S. foreign assistance program in the Philippines—technical assistance grants, loan funds, and food for peace under Public Law 480—were to be used in concert and would be coordinated with the inputs of such multilateral agencies as the United Nations Development Program, the Asia Development Bank, and the Consultative Group of Australia, Japan, Spain, and the United States, organized in 1970 under the chairmanship of the World Bank. While the multilateral lending agencies would take care of such larger projects as transportation, power generation, port improvement, and urban development, the U.S.-Philippine bilateral program was dedicated to the welfare of the little man. Americans gave substantial support to a dozen specific projects including land reform, feeder roads, irrigation systems, and practical research for small farmers, family planning, provision of potable drinking water, and electrification for the rural poor in the villages. Taken together these projects not only helped the needy but mounted a grass-roots attack on the sources of endemic insurgency. In the opinion of the President and Congress, they were worth the cost to the American taxpayer.[52]

Under President Carter, the United States each year will pass judgment on the wisdom and feasibility of the Foreign Assistance Program. The economic value to the Philippines of U.S. assistance is undeniable, but aid is an instrument of U.S. policy and theoretically will be extended to any government, totalitarian or otherwise, when it is considered to be in the American national interest. Continued foreign assistance to the Philippines is therefore a year-to-year proposition, with annual levels to be fixed by Congress. Secretary Kissinger once said that a dictatorial government's ability to field an army against Communist attack was not in itself sufficient proof of determined opposition to communism deserving of American aid, because the popular will and social justice were in the last analysis the essential underpinning of resistance to an external challenge. Nevertheless, he added that the

[52] Thomas C. Niblock, "The Small Farmer and the Rural Poor, Target of U.S. Economic Assistance to the Philippines" (Manila: U.S. Embassy, 1975). Niblock was director of the AID mission in Manila.

United States would continue to support governments to which it had made commitments even if they did not represent the popular will or provide social justice. American aid would be available where it had been promised—Washington would not renege on commitments it had made to unpopular dictatorships.[53]

This might have indicated to President Marcos that he was in no immediate danger of losing American aid. Yet he must have realized that any American economic commitment was *ex parte* and liable to be cut off at any time. Past performance was no guarantee that aid would be continued. For FY 1976 and FY 1977 the vote for aid to the Philippines was affirmative, recognizing that authoritarianism was a fact of life in developing countries, that it was beyond the power and responsibility of the United States to change it, and that it was still in the national interest to help the Philippines as an important and valued ally. But the Foreign Assistance Act of 1976 contained the same proviso that had been put into the Security Assistance Act denying assistance to governments guilty of a consistent pattern of gross violations of internationally recognized human rights, thus warning President Marcos that he was in danger of losing not only military assistance but also economic support.[54] The future of the American assistance program to the Philippines would depend on the U.S. government's judgment whether the lot of the people of the Philippines could be improved without perpetuating dictatorship and whether the security interest of the United States could be promoted without participating in the sacrifice of liberty.

Ending Special Relations. While the United States pondered the alternatives of foreign assistance, the government was under constant pressure to reappraise its policies of protecting American investments and promoting American commerce. Under the old system of special relations embodied in the Philippine Trade Act of 1946 and the Laurel-Langley agreement of 1954, American interests in the Philippines enjoyed the legal status of Philippine rather than foreign firms. Americans were given special rights with respect to public utilities and natural resources, exemption from the operation of nationalization laws, and some tariff preferences in the Philippines in return for compensatory preferences for Philippine products in the American market. These concessions had

---

[53] Secretary Kissinger's address before the Japan Society, New York City, June 18, 1975, issued as a press release by the Department of State.

[54] This fear of the loss of "aid" shows clearly why President Marcos is adamant on the payment of "rent" for the use of his military bases.

contributed in no small measure to the dominance of U.S. capital in the Philippines and had caused economic nationalists to whittle away at that dominance by means of national planning, import and exchange controls, and various administrative regulations for banking, mining, manufacturing, and commerce.

The imposition of martial law and the expiration of the Laurel-Langley agreement in 1974 brought to an end the old system of special relations which neither the United States nor the Philippines wished to perpetuate. The United States had no desire to use its political or economic power to dictate the direction of Philippine development and was quite amenable to the Philippines's becoming economically as well as politically independent, but within those limits, its objective was to see that under new circumstances, U.S. investors and traders would not be discriminated against and would be given the same opportunities as other investors and traders in fair and open competition.

Over the years, economic nationalism had grown more assertive in the Philippines. In the first flush of independence, the predominant ideal of the Filipino nationalist was to be as friendly to the United States as possible; a close tie with the United States was seen as the promise of a more prosperous future. Gradually the philosophy changed and laws were passed providing for the nationalization of the retail trade and for the encouragement of Filipino participation in investment activities and export trade. The champions of the Filipino First movement at the end of the fifties were for the most part conservative, pragmatic businessmen eager to seize economic advantages for Filipinos. Politically, they were identified with the government in contrast with the ideological, political nationalists among the insurgents and with student and labor radicals who were fanatically antiestablishment and anti-American. While the political nationalists were crying "Yankee Go Home," the economic nationalists appreciated the need for the American presence in the Philippines, but they wanted it under terms of Philippine control. They understood that if they were ever to achieve a take-off stage when the growth of their GNP would outstrip the appalling rate of population growth, they would have to guarantee a secure and predictable investment climate which could not be obtained if foreign investors were to fear nationalization or expropriation.

At the time of martial law, fifty major American companies and several hundred smaller ones represented about one-quarter of total assets and total sales in the Philippines. American interests were domi-

140

nant in banking, agriculture, mining, manufacturing, and the refining and distribution of petroleum. Other American firms ranging from blue jeans manufacturers to automobile producers were poised to enter the Philippine market where they could take advantage of their own capital, management skills, and technology as well as abundant resources, skilled labor, low wages, and a favorable economic climate.

Although Marcos wanted to encourage further investment to ensure the economic success of his regime, he could not disdain the demands of his economic nationalist supporters, whose goal was phased Filipinization. He softened the rules on minimum wages and repatriation of capital, but laid down restrictive regulations specifying the types of new investments he wanted. The government, penetrating ever deeper into the economic realm, laid down detailed rules for business operation which were subject to the constantly changing whims of the administration. For example, corporations were told how much of their product had to be exported and how much set aside for local consumption, how much investment had to be made in rice and corn production for their own workers, and what capital had to be earmarked for payment of fringe benefits for workers. Foreign banks were ordered to have ten dollars in local currency counterpart funds for every dollar of foreign capital, and foreign insurance companies were obliged to invest a certain proportion of their assets in government securities. Numerous restrictions were placed on local credits for foreign-owned companies. In spite of such rules and regulations, American individuals and corporations continued to do business in accordance with accepted Philippine customs, and they showed handsome profits. Net new investment was slow in coming—only $36 million in 1973 and $78 million in 1974, most of which was reinvestment of profits by established firms or expansion in the banking fields—and many of the marginal enterprises disposed of their equity to Filipino interests.

The crux of the problem of protection for American investors came with the expiration of the Laurel-Langley agreement in 1974. This affected American corporations, schools, religious organizations, and individuals who had acquired land and built wholly owned or majority-owned enterprises in accordance with parity privileges and were now forced to dispose of their land and to bring down their share of company ownership to the 40 percent limit specified in the Philippine constitution; it affected Americans who were about to be forced out of the retail trade and Americans who were about to be deprived of representation on boards of directors of enterprises in which they were minority stockholders. In addition to individual Americans who owned land for residential or industrial purposes in 1974, some sixty American companies held 13.8 million square meters of industrial, commercial, and other nonagricultural land, and five corporations held 12.9 million square meters of agricultural land, with a combined total value of $46 million.[55] Of 306 corporations in the Philippines with American equity in excess of 40 percent, 122 had real estate and land improvements valued at approximately $25 million and another 33 were engaged in the exploitation of natural resources or operation of public utilities with land and improvements valued at $8 million.[56]

President Marcos issued a series of decrees laying down rules for the disposition of rights acquired by American investors during the period parity had been in effect. He decreed that land of not more than 5,000 square meters in area could be held by private American individuals and could be transmitted to their heirs, but henceforth no more land at all could be purchased by Americans even for residential purposes. Corporations were given a reasonable time to submit plans for the transfer of their land holdings to Philippine entities and to dispose of their excess equity investments. They were encouraged to turn over their land to the National Development Company, some charitable organization, or a new corporation composed solely of their Filipino employees, with the right to lease the land back for a period of twenty-five years renewable for another twenty.[57] Further decrees provided that exemptions from the requirement of 100 percent Filipino ownership in the Retail Nationalization Law should be made for American companies engaged in manufacturing or processing and selling in bulk to an industrial or commercial user or to a service establishment or any restaurant affiliated with the hotel business. A final decree, modifying the old prohibition of foreigners on boards of directors or in top management positions, permitted foreign representation on boards of directors in proportion to foreign equity in companies engaged in businesses that must, however, be Filipino controlled.

These arrangements were pragmatic and resulted from ten years of dialogue between Marcos and private U.S. interests in the Philippines

---

[55] *Philippine Times,* Chicago, May 16-31, 1975.
[56] *American Chamber of Commerce in the Philippines,* News Release, January 8, 1973.
[57] *Far Eastern Economic Review,* April 25, 1975.

with regard to their respective demands and requirements. The U.S. Embassy in Manila was a concerned but passive participant in the discussions, making no effort to exert pressure, but using its influence in seeking justice and equal protection for Americans under Philippine law—nothing more. Marcos succeeded in steering a middle course, requiring U.S. business to formally comply with the provisions of the constitution while allowing enough latitude that Americans would still feel welcome in the Philippines. His decrees reflected his wish to preserve a hospitable climate for further foreign loans and investments without compromising his long-range goal of Filipinization. Any further transfers of American rights of ownership would in all likelihood be gradual, not abrupt, and no extensive nationalization or expropriation without due compensation appeared to be imminent. It was apparent, however, that none of Marcos's decrees contained any guarantee of permanence and they could easily be changed to the advantage of the Philippines in bargaining for a new economic treaty or more favorable conditions of trade.

The essence of economic bargaining after the expiration of the Laurel-Langley agreement was the conflict between the American objective of securing the best possible conditions for its investors and traders within the framework of normal international economic relationships and the Philippine desire to promote the best interests of its own businessmen by means of continued special preferences, if possible. Negotiations were complicated by differing interpretations of special relations, a phrase connoting one thing to the Americans and quite another to the Filipinos. The American concept of special relations as applied to the Philippines was different from that which linked the United States and Great Britain, for example, where the ties were cultural and ideological as well as diplomatic and strategic. Special relations with the Philippines stemmed only from the colonial experience and its aftermath: the feeling that the United States bore some responsibility for the security and welfare of the Philippines and for the survival of the way of life and political ideals that the Americans had endeavored to bring to the Philippines. It did not imply any sense of obligation to fight for the Philippines or any wish to continue the system of mutual economic advantages, which had been worked out to protect the American economic stake in the Philippines and to ease the difficulties of the new nation in its transition to independence.

The Philippine view was very different. Holding the United States responsible for their low standard of living and economic difficulties, the Filipinos felt that the Americans had a continuing obligation to assist in their development. In the Philippines, special relations had a double meaning: broadly, the term was applied to the whole range of close political, economic, and ideological ties that the Filipinos assumed were inherent in the patron-client relationship; narrowly, it referred to the system of special preference in trade and investments that had existed since the colonial period. It had been formalized in the Tariff Act of 1909, the Tydings-McDuffie Act of 1934, the Bell Trade Act of 1946, and the Laurel-Langley agreement of 1954. Because the fine distinctions were often disregarded, the Philippines exhibited a curious ambivalence in discussing special relations with the United States. Sometimes the Philippine representatives disclaimed any desire to continue special relations on the grounds that as a mature, independent country, the Philippines wanted equal treatment, no more, no less. At other times, the Filipinos insinuated that they were entitled to special consideration as a consequence of their historic dependence on the United States. On the one hand, the phrase special relations was occasionally used to seek favors that were conceived to be the rightful due of the Philippines; on the other, it was scorned as being out of tune with the new spirit of respectable independence and was openly condemned as the device by which the Americans had exploited the Philippines. It made no difference which tack the Philippine government was inclined to follow in 1974, the American government was determined to end special relations and to reject any trade-off of special treatment for American business in the Philippines against special treatment for Filipinos in the American market. Any bargains would have to be made in accordance with the system of general preferences and within the provisions of the General Agreement on Trade and Tariffs.

Negotiations for the replacement of the Laurel-Langley agreement began in 1967, but they made practically no progress in view of the fact that the vital issue—the control of trade—lay ultimately in the hands of Congress, beyond the competence of those representing the executive branch.[58] Since economic discussions were often over-

---

[58] Laura Jeanine Henze, "U.S.-Philippine Economic Relations and Trade Negotiations," *Asian Survey,* April 1976, pp. 319-338.

shadowed by simultaneous negotiations on mutual security, the future of the bases, and military assistance, it was impossible to reach agreement on terms for a treaty of amity and commerce or a treaty of economic cooperation and development.

The expiration of the Laurel-Langley agreement did little damage to U.S. trade with the Philippines but dealt a serious blow to the Philippines which lost its quotas and other tariff preferences in the U.S. market. Such Philippine products as copra, abaca, logs, chromite, copper concentrates, and gold did not suffer without benefit of preference since they were placed on the American free list. Other products such as coconut oil, pineapples, plywood veneers, copra meal, embroideries, and scrap tobacco were subject only to light duty and could probably maintain their import levels. But the loss of the sugar quota was disastrous. In 1975 sugar was expensive and in short supply, so the passing of the Laurel-Langley agreement was scarcely noticed. But in 1976 when the bottom dropped out of the sugar market the Philippine government, which had practically taken over every step in the sugar trade, found itself with perhaps as much as $1 billion tied up in unmarketed surplus and without hope of relief from the United States.[59] Furthermore, the Philippines faced a duty of one cent a pound on coconut oil, while competing vegetable and palm oils entered the United States duty free, and a heavier duty on Philippine mahogany than on woods from other underdeveloped countries because Marcos had refused to participate in early discussions of general tariff preferences for goods from all underdeveloped countries. When it became clear that the Philippines was not going to be granted further special preferences, Marcos said he felt aggrieved because of the undue delay in amending what he called unequal treatment,[60] but his only hope for more favorable consideration for Philippine products in the U.S. market was to seek coverage for as many as possible under the general preference scheme and to negotiate most-favored-nation tariff reductions with the United States on a bilateral basis.

In contrast to the solution of the problems of American investors in the Philippines that was effected by decrees of the Philippine president, the settlement of U.S.-Philippine problems of trade was accomplished by the American Congress through the Trade Act and the

---

[59] George McArthur, *San Francisco Chronicle*, December 2, 1976.
[60] *U.S. News and World Report*, November 22, 1976.

Sugar Act of 1974. The Trade Act brought the system of special preferences for the Philippines to an end in favor of general preferences
for all underdeveloped countries, and the Sugar Act did away with all
quotas for imported sugar. The only sop to the Philippines was a waiver
in the Trade Act making possible some limited special preferences for
the Philippines if the Philippines would first agree to give favorable
treatment to Americans in the Philippines. Since no such agreement was
in prospect, ordinary trade between the two countries was to continue
without benefit of an underlying commercial convention, subject only
to the conditions and regulations applying to any two countries participating in normal international commerce.

Mounting Psychological Tensions

The protracted discussion of mutual security issues and economic relations exposed deep differences of opinion due to conflicts of national
interests and sometimes aggravated by clashes between individuals.
Misconceptions and misunderstandings had produced bad feelings as
well as political disagreement. Americans were frequently accused of
arrogance, condescension, or inertia, while the Filipinos were thought
to be hypersensitive, opportunistic, and aggressive. In the past, irritation
had not disrupted the smooth course of good relations, but in the future,
as psychological tensions mounted, negotiations promised to be more
difficult—all the more in that nationalism in the Philippines and the
concern for human rights in the United States were on the rise.

Philippine Nationalism and Anti-Americanism. Criticism of the United
States or its policies, often referred to in the Philippines as anti-
Americanism, was as old as the American presence in the Philippines.
Aguinaldo and his *insurrectos* were anti-American in the sense that
they objected to the substitution of the United States for Spain as an
alien ruler. Quezon, Osmena, and their Nacionalista followers were
obliged to be anti-American in their struggle for independence. But
the anti-Americanism of the colonial period was a matter of political
difference rather than personal hatred, never reaching crisis proportions
because of the American promise of independence upon the establishment of stable government.

The anti-Americanism of the early leaders of the independence
movement, often based on jealousy and opportunism, differed greatly

from the anti-Americanism of the liberal intellectuals and the Socialists, who from the beginning condemned the United States for doing too much for the rich and powerful and not enough for the underprivileged. In their minds, Americans were inseparably linked with the native oligarchy, and criticism of the one automatically implicated the other. This criticism was mild in tone and insignificant in effect during the colonial period because of the overwhelming popular acceptance of the American presence among the masses. Very few Filipinos indeed found reason to be dissatisfied with the United States.

After World War II, on the eve of independence, the exhilaration of victory and the demonstration of American willingness to assist the Philippines in its hour of greatest need forestalled anti-Americanism on the part of the Philippine government but not on the part of the Huks and dissident liberals who felt that the United States was imposing a new and more subtle imperialism on the Philippines. As the domestic troubles of the Philippines increased, however, anti-American sentiments proliferated among government officials, who came to feel that the United States was doing too little to help the Philippines and too late. The Americans were accused of selfish motives in giving military and economic assistance and in refusing to go further in providing for Philippine security. The Americans were also blamed for failing to recognize and bear the consequences of their own shortcomings when they had been sovereign in the Philippines.

Anti-Americanism subsided as the internal situation improved and practically disappeared during the era of good feeling in the first years of President Magsaysay. But with the latter part of the Magsaysay and the Garcia administrations, both of them Nacionalista, anti-Americanism became an article of political faith, inextricably linked with ultra-nationalistic political and economic demands. Many members of the rising middle class joined the chorus of anti-Americanism because, as technocrats and new managers, they coveted the jobs and enterprises of the Americans. The ranks of the rising middle class were split, however; the prosperity of large numbers of Filipino lawyers and business-men depended upon their American connections. Anti-Americanism on the part of outstanding Philippine political and economic leaders often reflected their own personal interests, but journalists and intellectuals consistently were ardent advocates of the ideology of Filipino First. Dissidents in the countryside continued to be anti-American, anticapital, and antigovernment.

147

Anti-Americanism in the late fifties rose and fell as the internal situation in the Philippines showed signs of sickness or health and as American assistance was judged to be ample or inadequate. No matter how much the media castigated the Americans and the policies of the United States, however, anti-Americanism never reached the masses, for whom the American image was as bright as ever. Students, liberals, workers, Huks, and Socialists were never able to attract genuine mass support and to unite with ultranationalistic writers, politicians, and technocrats in an integrated anti-American movement. Anti-Americanism was still less an affair of the heart than one of political strategy and economic advantage, and was not sufficiently strong to interrupt the smooth flow of Philippine-American relations. On the official level, the bonds between the two countries remained deep, strong, and, in the view of both, necessary, while on the personal level no matter how much the Filipinos said they hated the United States, the U.S.A. was where they liked to go and send their children to be educated.

Under the Liberal administration of Macapagal, while Marcos was in the Senate, nationalism remained strong but it was less anti-American. Nationalism and friendly ties with the United States were not thought of as mutually exclusive as long as the United States was accepted as a protector against the U.S.S.R., China, and possibly a revived and remilitarized Japan. With the advent of Marcos, the new standard bearer for the Nacionalistas, to the presidency and with the multiplication of American troubles in Vietnam, anti-Americanism in the Philippines took a new twist. It was no longer focused exclusively on aspects of bilateral relations but was extended to cover the whole range of American global policies. Whereas the Americans previously had enjoyed the unqualified endorsement of the Philippines for its cold war containment of communism, the course of developments in Vietnam stirred up increasing resentment and skepticism in the Philippines. As the Philippines slipped toward chaos and bankruptcy at the end of Marcos's first term, Marcos adopted a tone of respect toward President Johnson and the American Congress, but he did not hesitate to lash out against the United States for failing to bring peace and stability in Southeast Asia. No longer blaming the Communists exclusively for the suffering of Asia, he censured the United States and other affluent powers for doing too little to assist the small nations in their struggle to overcome the conditions in which Communist insurgency could flourish.

He chided the United States for trying to become the policeman of the world and suggested that it should do more to help its friends fight their own battles in their own way.

Ambivalent, President Marcos retained an air of cordiality in his contacts with the United States, but he did not mitigate his public criticism of American policies. He made no effort to curb anti-American outbursts on the floor of the Philippine Congress or in the columns of the press. Such outbursts served his political purposes. Confident that the United States needed him more than he needed the United States, he believed that the United States, unwilling to risk another Vietnam, could not afford to deny him anything he might demand in his fight against the insurgents. He pointed out that the insurgents were far more anti-American than he and his government of oligarchs could ever be. The Americans felt as much displeasure over his ambivalence as he felt over their ineffectiveness. They did not want the Philippines to go down the Communist drain, so to speak, and they feared what might lie ahead if the political deterioration that had marked President Marcos's first administration should grow progressively worse. Acknowledging that the destiny of the United States in the Philippines was linked to the existence of a strong, viable government in Manila, the Americans were inclined to attach more importance to his pro-American than to his anti-American side. They were not willing, however, to be backed into a corner where Marcos or any other Philippine leader could dictate their options.

With the imposition of martial law, President Marcos gave full rein to the spirit of Philippine nationalism. Although he alone was the unchallenged spokesman for the Philippine people, it was clear that whatever regime might follow him would in all likelihood be equally adamant in its diplomatic dealing with the United States. He could afford to be intransigent in his demands and uncompromising in his attitudes regardless of the psychological tensions that would result. His speeches reflected his firmness, and his actions occasionally underscored his determination to be completely independent of the United States. In 1976 when an earthquake rocked the Philippines, Marcos refused offers of American aid, and when a light plane crashed killing six diplomats including three Americans, he refused for six days to permit the U.S. air force to launch a search for the missing pasengers. [61]

---

[61] Ibid.

Ideological Barriers to Good Will. American irritation over Philippine nationalism was matched by Philippine resentment of American criticism of martial law. The Philippines felt that domestic affairs were none of America's business, but the United States insisted that if it was to help the Philippines it had a right to concern itself with the nature of the government with which it dealt. The United States wanted the good will of the Philippines, but not at the cost of destroying the foundation on which that good will had been nurtured.

The American government worked diligently to improve the image of the United States in the Philippines and to make its policies more palatable. Its public relations agency overseas, the United States Information Service (USIS), maintained a library of books and periodicals reflecting America's tastes and intellectual interests, conducted a cultural exchange program bringing artists, speakers, professors, and athletic teams to the Philippines and providing support for thousands of Filipino students in the United States, and was responsible for the Voice of America as well as pamphlets and press releases intended to publicize U.S. foreign policies and clarify American points of view. The mission of USIS was to make as much information as possible about the United States available to Filipinos, on the assumption that deeper understanding would promote good will.

American good will toward the Philippines rested on a narrow base. Most Americans knew very little about the Philippines. Few college courses covered Philippine affairs and almost none in the grade schools even touched upon them; few books were written about the Philippines and none achieved mass circulation; the Philippines seldom made the movies or prime viewing time on television. The daily press carried little news about the Philippines and such items as appeared tended to be circulated through syndicated metropolitan papers or the wire services, so that Americans in New York, Atlanta, or San Francisco were exposed to precisely the same information. Very little editorial opinion was expressed on policies toward the Philippines.

Good will between the United States and the Philippines thrived on personal contacts. American residents in the Philippines, tourists, or sailors with weekend passes invariably enjoyed the warm hospitality and infectious good humor of the Filipinos and some 500,000 Filipinos made the United States their home. President Marcos said he was less

150

concerned about the intrusion of China and the Soviet Union into Philippine affairs than about the Filipinos in the United States. Some Filipinos living in the United States were staunch defenders of Marcos, saying that he had done away not with democracy but with its distortions and that he had given the Philippines a new status and a new dignity. Others, including some distinguished Filipino citizens with long records of supporting both democratic government and friendship with the United States went so far as to urge the United States to cut off all forms of assistance to the Philippines as long as Marcos remained in power. Feeling that any dictatorship, whatever its virtues, was worse than any democracy, they did not wish in any way to condone the destruction of a political way of life that they had helped to create.[62]

The debate between Filipinos in the United States on the faults and merits of martial law had its counterpart in arguments between Americans. Those Americans who expressed approval of martial law felt that order was essential to the search for prosperity and stability in the Philippines. They were concerned with the preservation of freedom and civil rights but not to the extent of sacrificing security for the preservation of a democratic government. Their counsel was that the United States should seek accommodation with Marcos lest he, or the nation without him, take a less tolerant stand towards America's economic and military interests in the Philippines. That counsel prevailed as long as President Ford was in the White House.

While President Ford remained silent, neither condemning nor approving President Marcos, that segment of the American public interested in Philippine affairs expressed increasing resentment over the Filipinos' criticism of the American failure in Indochina and pointed out that the Filipinos had done practically nothing to prevent a catastrophe that was as damaging to the Philippines as to the United States. The more Filipino tempers flared, the angrier Americans became. The more strongly the Filipinos argued their case, the more the American replies hardened. A tinge of bitterness added to the strain of negotiations, and emotions deepened with the continued flouting of democratic ideals by President Marcos's authoritarian regime.

Frequent references to the violation of human rights on the floor of the Congress reflected a growing American concern for the future of civil liberties in the Philippines. Catholic newspapers in the

---

[62] These conflicts of opinion are discernible in the references cited in footnotes 40 and 41.

Philippines were closed, American priests deported for subversive activities, and the Manila head of the Associated Press News Bureau expelled. On April 7, 1976, an editorial in the *Washington Star* urged that it was time to "stop catering to tin horn dictators," and on Philippine independence day, June 12, 1976, Senator McGovern called for a drastic change in America's Philippine policy.[63]

An American historian knowledgeable in Philippine affairs, wrote in mid-1976 that it was time to stop Machiavellian diplomacy and go back to basics—fidelity to our own highest principles. Describing support of the Marcos regime as morally bankrupt and tactically foolish, he said the United States should not lament the passing of a corrupt democracy but should not tie itself to President Marcos either.[64] The attitudes of congressmen and senators debating military and nonmilitary assistance to the Philippines have already been noted.

A new factor affected the debate when Jimmy Carter in the course of his campaign took a strong stand for human rights and the Democratic platform endorsed his position. After his inauguration, President Carter reaffirmed his commitment to human rights and let it be known that his dedication to principles would play a large part in determining his foreign policy.

In commenting on Carter's view of U.S. relations with Asia, President Marcos said he foresaw no substantial change in American policy and definitely expected that the United States would try increasingly to anchor those relations in mutual trust, respect, and equality.[65] But it must have been perfectly plain that if good will were to continue in spite of the tensions that had been growing for a decade, American concessions to Philippine nationalism would have to be matched by Philippine recognition of deep and growing American concern for the fate of democratic ideals, civil liberties, and human rights in the Philippines.

---

[63] Occurrences such as these are given extensive coverage in the anti-Marcos *Philippine News,* San Francisco. The address of Senator McGovern appears on page S9643 of the *Congressional Record,* June 16, 1976, and the expulsion of the A.P. Bureau Chief was reported in the *Philippine News,* November 20-26, 1976. The closing of the Catholic papers and the expulsion of American priests were reported in the issue of December 4-10, 1976.

[64] Peter W. Stanley, "America and the Conservative Revolution in the Philippines," *Harvard Magazine,* May 1976.

[65] *Agence France Presse,* Hong Kong, December 11, 1976 as quoted in *Foreign Broadcast Information Service, Asia and the Pacific,* December 13, 1976.

DATE DUE